BEST JUDO

BEST JUDO

Isao Inokuma   Nobuyuki Sato

KODANSHA INTERNATIONAL
Tokyo • New York • London

Action photos by Keizō Kaneko; demonstration photos by Yoshinao Murai.

Distributed in the United States by Kodansha America, Inc., 575 Lexington Avenue, New York, N.Y. 10022, and in the United KIngdom and continetal Europe by Kodansha Europe Ltd., 95 Aldwych, London WC2B 4JF.

Published by Kodansha International Ltd., 17-14 Otowa 1-chome, Bunkyo-ku Tokyo 112-8652, and Kodansha America, Inc. Copyright © 1979 by Kodansha International Ltd. All rights reserved. Printed in Japan.

LCC 79-84656
ISBN 0-87011-786-6
ISBN 4-7700-1286-1 (in Japan)

First edition, 1979
First paperback edition, 1986
02 03 04 05   20 19 18 17 16 15

www.thejapanpage.com

Contents

Left to right: Dr. Shigeyoshi Matsumae (Chairman of the Board of Trustees and President of Tokai University, President of International Budo University, and President of the International Judo Federation); the authors, Isao Inokuma and Nobuyuki Sato; and Yasuhiro Yamashita (winner of the All-Japan Judo Championship, 1977–85).

Foreword

Shigeyoshi Matsumae
President, Tokai University

It is wonderful to see how popular Kodokan judo has become throughout the world today. I would like to congratulate Isao Inokuma and Nobuyuki Sato on their timely instruction book, *Best Judo,* which has been designed for judo enthusiasts in all the countries of the world. It is a book I have been looking forward to, for I have long felt Inokuma and Sato to be among the best qualified to speak on the real spirit and techniques of judo. For those who follow the sport, these two men need no introduction. They are both former All-Japan judo champions and have excellent international reputations, having won titles in the Olympic Games, in World Judo Tournaments, and in other international contests. Today, as instructors at Tokai University, they are uncovering and training many top-class judoists. One of their students is Yasuhiro Yamashita, who won the coveted All-Japan title at the age of only 19. The authors' outstanding records, experience, leadership, enthusiasm, and numerous activities, including books like this one, have indeed made them into a major force for the popularization of judo on an international scale.

Judo is a representative Japanese sport which has an international character. Constituting a culture in itself, judo is contributing enormously to friendship and peace among the nations of the world today by offering an area in which people can come together for fruitful exchange. In this way, judo is helping to promote the happiness and prosperity of all mankind. This is judo's mission and there can be no loftier goal.

Inokuma and Sato are two men who fully understand this role that judo has to play. They are judoists who are capable of bringing the ideals of judo into actuality. *Best Judo* incorporates all their experience and studies in judo, and I am confident that it will make a strong impression on judo enthusiasts everywhere.

My joy will know no bounds if, through this book, the readers come to know what this subtle art of self-defense really is, not only its techniques, but its spirit. I would like those who use this book to understand the object of their training and, through judo, widen the circle of their friendships and contribute to international peace and goodwill.

In conclusion, I would like again to compliment Isao Inokuma and Nobuyuki Sato on their efforts in writing this book. I recommend their work highly to judoists throughout the world.

Preface

Isao Inokuma

Judo today is an international sport knowing no boundary between states or races. It is a sport in which millions of people throughout the world are engaged, whether for simple recreation or for more serious purposes. The world-wide popularity of judo is evidenced by the more than one hundred nations that belong to the International Judo Federation, by the acceptance of judo as an Olympic event, and by the numerous international judo contests held each year, such as the World Judo Tournament.

Several decades ago, judo was considered a sport in which only the Japanese could excel. But with the international character of the sport today, the performances of judoists from various countries have improved considerably and show a skill and power on a par with that of their Japanese counterparts. Geesink and Ruska of the Netherlands and Novikov of the Soviet Union, for example, have already surpassed Japanese judoists to become Olympic or world champions. Their accomplishments clearly show that judo is no longer a monopoly of Japan but a common property of the entire world. That judoists from many nations are training hard to perfect their spirits and techniques can only help stimulate the further spread and development of judo.

As a man brought up in the judo world, I take pride in seeing how Jigoro Kano-sensei's sport has become so popular since its organization a hundred years ago. And I have made it my mission to see that the spirit of judo, through correct understanding of its principles, becomes as widely practiced as the sport itself.

I am grateful that I have been given an opportunity to take one step toward this goal through the publication of *Best Judo,* written by Nobuyuki Sato and myself. Sato, like me, is devoted to the internationalization of judo and the judo spirit.

The judo presented in this book is that which is recognized by the Kodokan, the official judo organization in Japan. Covered here are the fundamental and representative techniques performed from a standing posture, while on the mat, and in combination. Judo is practiced by many people for pure recreation because it is a satisfying and intelligent sport. It should be pointed out, however, that judo is a systematic sport and that judo practice techniques and strategies like those in this book all derive from the Kodokan rules governing organized tournament competition. By confining your practice to the techniques presented here you will avoid injury and be able to practice fairly with other judoists anywhere. If the opportunity presents itself we would like in the future to write a more advanced and technical work that focuses on some of the high-level techniques that are also frequently used.

In order to help the reader understand judo quickly we have relied on action-sequence photos instead of voluminous text explanations. The models for the photos are, aside from Sato and myself, Hideharu Shirase, Katsuhiko Kashiwazaki, Katsumi Suzuki, and Yasuhiro Yamashita, all of whom are representative judoists of Japan. These men have trained under us and have achieved brilliant records in competition. We hope that the reader will be able to grasp the vital points of the various judo techniques presented here by carefully studying each photo. We have also allocated a substantial number of pages in the book to physical training methods and to essays on judo. We believe that the fostering of basic physical power is a prerequisite for modern judoists, and we hope that our impressions of judo may be of interest and help to our readers in numerous ways.

In order to become strong in judo there is only mastery of the fundamentals and hard training every day. Everyone starts training by learning the basic movements of judo such as posture and how to be thrown. You will be thrown to the mat innumerable times during your training, but the time will eventually come when you will at last be able to throw your opponent. There is no one who is able to throw his opponent or hold him down with a mat technique from the beginning. We would like to recommend that you keep this always in mind and train hard to master the fundamentals as soon as possible. The importance of a teacher cannot be overrated. But if no teacher is available to you, try to attend judo contests or watch them on television whenever they appear.

The techniques of judo are limitless and the spirit of judo is sublime. All the countries in the world have their own particular fighting arts, and it is our opinion that from now on we judoists must make a comprehensive study of these arts together with the study of our own sport.

Readers coming to judo for the first time may be dismayed at the original Japanese judo terms used in this book. These terms are used here because they have gained wide acceptance throughout the world as the language of judo. English equivalents are, however, given at the first appearance in the text, in the glossary and indexes, or in the major text headings.

We would like to express our thanks to the organizations and individuals that helped us: the Kodokan, the Matsumae Young People's Judo School, the Tokai University Judo Club, Toshiaki Hashimoto, Hideharu Shirase, Katsuhiko Kashiwazaki, Katsumi Suzuki, and Yasuhiro Yamashita. We would also like to thank the staff of Kodansha International for their encouragement and advice.

1

Judo
Fundamentals

People who see judo contests at an arena or on television marvel at the grace and the fluidity of judo techniques or at the speed and energy of the throws. What they don't see is the hard trainings and sometimes repetitive workouts that judoists undertake over many years to bring their techniques to perfection. Judo techniques don't just happen. They are carefully worked out, practiced combinations of basic movements, postures, and holds. This chapter presents these basics and introduces some techniques that will help you get used to the mat.

Shizen hontai

Migi shizentai

Hidari shizentai

Jigo hontai

Migi jigotai

Hidari jigotai

Posture

The basic posture in judo is the natural posture, or *shizentai*. This simply means that you stand in a natural way. From *shizentai* you can move into various other postures.

There are three natural postures—*shizen hontai* (basic natural posture), *migi shizentai* (right natural posture), and *hidari shizentai* (left natural posture).

Jigotai, or defensive posture, is taken by spreading the feet a bit wider than in *shizentai* and bending both knees to lower the body's center of gravity. *Jigotai* also has three forms—*jigo hontai* (basic defensive posture), *migi jigotai* (right defensive posture), and *hidari jigotai* (left defensive posture). *Jigotai* is used when defending yourself from the opponent's attack and is not very effective for attacking. If you must assume this posture for a time to defend yourself, be sure to switch back to *shizentai* as soon as you can.

All attack and defense techniques derive from postures. It is extremely important, therefore, that you maintain correct posture at all times.

SHIZENTAI : natural posture

SHIZEN HONTAI: Spread both heels about 30 centimeters (1 ft.) apart. Point the toes of your feet naturally outward and place the weight of your body equally on both feet. Your knees and hips should be relaxed so that you can, at any time, step freely forward or backward. This is the fundamental judo posture.

MIGI SHIZENTAI: From *shizen hontai*, move your right foot forward about 30 centimeters (1 ft.).

HIDARI SHIZENTAI: From *shizen hontai*, move your left foot forward about 30 centimeters (1 ft.).

JIGOTAI : defensive posture

JIGO HONTAI: Stand with both feet a bit wider apart than in *shizen hontai*. Bend your knees to lower your hips.

MIGI JIGOTAI: Take one step forward from *jigo hontai* with your right leg.

HIDARI JIGOTAI: Take one step forward from *jigo hontai* with your left leg.

1

Entering seiza   1

2

2

3   4

Salutation

Judo practice takes the form of a fight. But no matter how fierce the practice may be, its object is to improve your technique and train your spirit. As a reflection of these higher goals, all judoists pay due respect to each other both before and after the practice or actual contest. There are two salutations in judo; one is made standing (*ritsurei*) and the other, kneeling (*zarei*). The combatants stand or sit about 3.6 meters (almost 12 ft.) apart. In the explanations that follow, the bold numbers in the text correspond to the photo numbers.

3

Standing salutation

STANDING SALUTATION

1. Stand with your heels together and your toes open outward.

2, 3. Tuck your chin in and, with a natural motion, bend your upper body forward about 30°. Touch your fingertips to your kneecaps. This takes about 4 seconds. Then return to your original posture.

Seated salutation

FROM A STANDING POSTURE TO A SEATED POSTURE

1. Start in an upright posture.

2. Pull back your left leg and kneel down on your knee (keep the tips of your toes upright on the floor).

3. Kneel down on your right knee and place both feet together.

4. Straighten out your toes and squat down with your right big toe crossing the left big toe. The space between both your knees should be about 20 centimeters (8 in.). Place both hands on your thighs, the fingers together and turned slightly inward. This position is called *seiza*. When standing up, follow the same steps in reverse.

1

KNEELING SALUTATION

1. Begin in *seiza* with your hands on your lap.

2, 3. Place your hands in front of your knees on the floor and bend your upper body forward. When bowing, don't raise your hips or bend and lower your elbows. The index fingers of both hands should be facing each other and should be about 6 centimeters (2½ in.) apart. The upper body should be bent down so that the brow of your head is about 30 centimeters (1 ft.) above both hands. Return to *seiza*.

2

Right hold
from *migi shizentai*

Left hold
from *hidari shizentai*

Right hold
from *migi jigotai*

Left hold
from *hidari jigotai*

Holding Methods

The basic holds in judo are taken from *shizentai* (natural posture) and *jigotai* (defensive posture) by grasping the lapel of the opponent's jacket with one hand and his sleeve with the other. There are many variations of the basic holds, such as a double-lapel grip or a double-sleeve grip. When holding the opponent, put strength in your ring and little fingers, and let your thumb rest lightly on the fabric of the jacket. Grips used in competitive situations to gain control of the opponent are called *kenka yotsu,* and many of these are shown in the photographs in the following chapters. With a partner, practice holds appropriate to your body size, strength, agility, and favorite techniques.

Tsukuri and Kake

Tsukuri is the entry and proper fitting of your body into the position taken just before the moment required for completion of your throwing technique. Necessarily, the off-balancing (*kuzushi,* see below) of your opponent takes place at the same time as *tsukuri* so that he is helpless and easily controlled. *Kake* is the completing movement of your technique.

Judo techniques work splendidly when these three elements work together almost instantaneously to become a single entity. If any one of them is inadequate or late in coming, your attempt to throw the opponent or bring him down to the mat will likely end in failure.

Kuzushi

Kuzushi (literally, breaking) in judo means forcing the opponent into an unbalanced position. This is an important factor in executing effective *nagewaza* (throwing techniques), for when the opponent is off-balance he is unable to use his strength aggressively and is virtually under your control. *Kuzushi* can be performed in eight different directions (*happo no kuzushi*). Although you can use a variety of techniques, such as pushing, pulling, or going around the opponent, you should always execute *kuzushi* not with your hands alone but with your entire body. You must also consider the distance between you and your opponent.

1 **2** **3**

Yoko ukemi from a squatting posture

4 **5**

Yoko ukemi from a standing posture

1 **2** **3** **4**

YOKO UKEMI : falling sideways
FROM A SQUATTING POSTURE

1, 2, 3. From a squatting or half-rising posture, raise your right arm up to the level of your left shoulder. At the same time kick out your right leg diagonally to the left front.

4. Drop your buttocks to the mat and roll back to the right side.

5. Tuck in your chin and strike the mat with your right arm. Keep your left hand lightly on your belt.

Similar movements can be used for *yoko ukemi* to the left. Practice falls to both sides.

FROM A STANDING POSTURE

1. Assume a standing posture.

2. Advance your left foot one step diagonally to the left.

3. Kick out your right foot to the left front and let your body drop to the mat.

4. Hit the mat with your right arm.

Mae ukemi

1 *Mae-mawari ukemi* **2** **3** **4**

1 **2** **3** **4**

MAE UKEMI : *falling forward*

1, 2. Assume a standing posture and fall forward.

3. Keep both hands at a 45° angle to the floor and let them form a V-shape pointing out from your body.

4. Hit the mat with both arms; support your body with arms and toes.

MAE-MAWARI UKEMI : *tumbling forward*

1. From *migi shizentai,* bend down and place your right hand on the mat, between your legs and with the fingers pointing inward.

2. Kick out with your left leg and roll your body forward.

3. During your fall, your right elbow, right shoulder, left hip, and body make a circle as they contact the mat one after the other along a diagonal line.

4. When your left hip is about to touch the mat, strike the mat strongly with your left hand. The angle between your left hand and your body should be about 30°. Place your right hand lightly on your belt.

A similar procedure is followed for *mae-mawari ukemi* to the left.

POINTERS : A regular triangle is formed by your left hand, right foot, and left foot. Your right hand is placed in the middle of the triangle. The backs of your left and right hands should be facing upward and the fingers pointing inward. Place your right ear against your right shoulder.

Placement of the hands and feet

One-handed tumble **1** **2** **3**

4 **5** **6**

Ushiro ukemi   Yoko ukemi   Mae-mawari ukemi

ONE-HANDED TUMBLE

1. Advance forward, speeding up gradually.

2. Step forward onto your left foot.

3. Place your left hand on the mat in front and, pushing off with your left foot, do a big somersault.

4, 5. Just before your right hip hits the mat, strike the mat strongly with your right hand.

6. Then rise up into *shizen hontai.*

UKEMI PRACTICE

When you have mastered the basics of the various *ukemi,* practice them while you are in motion, or with a partner or an obstacle. The important thing is for you to learn to execute *ukemi* correctly no matter what way you fall.

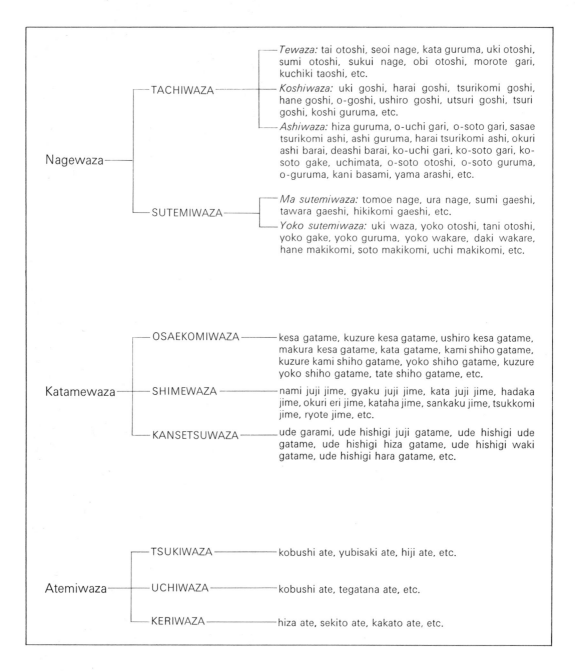

- **Nagewaza**
  - **TACHIWAZA**
    - *Tewaza:* tai otoshi, seoi nage, kata guruma, uki otoshi, sumi otoshi, sukui nage, obi otoshi, morote gari, kuchiki taoshi, etc.
    - *Koshiwaza:* uki goshi, harai goshi, tsurikomi goshi, hane goshi, o-goshi, ushiro goshi, utsuri goshi, tsuri goshi, koshi guruma, etc.
    - *Ashiwaza:* hiza guruma, o-uchi gari, o-soto gari, sasae tsurikomi ashi, ashi guruma, harai tsurikomi ashi, okuri ashi barai, deashi barai, ko-uchi gari, ko-soto gari, ko-soto gake, uchimata, o-soto otoshi, o-soto guruma, o-guruma, kani basami, yama arashi, etc.
  - **SUTEMIWAZA**
    - *Ma sutemiwaza:* tomoe nage, ura nage, sumi gaeshi, tawara gaeshi, hikikomi gaeshi, etc.
    - *Yoko sutemiwaza:* uki waza, yoko otoshi, tani otoshi, yoko gake, yoko guruma, yoko wakare, daki wakare, hane makikomi, soto makikomi, uchi makikomi, etc.

- **Katamewaza**
  - **OSAEKOMIWAZA** — kesa gatame, kuzure kesa gatame, ushiro kesa gatame, makura kesa gatame, kata gatame, kami shiho gatame, kuzure kami shiho gatame, yoko shiho gatame, kuzure yoko shiho gatame, tate shiho gatame, etc.
  - **SHIMEWAZA** — nami juji jime, gyaku juji jime, kata juji jime, hadaka jime, okuri eri jime, kataha jime, sankaku jime, tsukkomi jime, ryote jime, etc.
  - **KANSETSUWAZA** — ude garami, ude hishigi juji gatame, ude hishigi ude gatame, ude hishigi hiza gatame, ude hishigi waki gatame, ude hishigi hara gatame, etc.

- **Atemiwaza**
  - **TSUKIWAZA** — kobushi ate, yubisaki ate, hiji ate, etc.
  - **UCHIWAZA** — kobushi ate, tegatana ate, etc.
  - **KERIWAZA** — hiza ate, sekito ate, kakato ate, etc.

Judo Techniques

There are many kinds of techniques in judo, but they can all be classified into three main categories: *nagewaza* (throwing techniques), *katamewaza* or *newaza* (grappling techniques on the mat), and *atemiwaza* (striking techniques). *Nagewaza* and *katamewaza* are also called *randoriwaza* (techniques for free practice) and are used both in practice sessions and contests. *Atemiwaza* are used to strike or kick the opponent's vital points. Because they are dangerous if used in free practice, *atemiwaza* are practiced only in controlled model techniques, what are called *kata*.

2
Throwing Techniques

Throwing techniques are called nagewaza. In a judo contest a well-executed throw that sends the opponent to the mat can earn the thrower a solid ippon (one point), which is all that is needed for victory. Within nagewaza are tachi-waza (throwing techniques involving the hand, hip, or leg) and sute-miwaza (in which you throw the opponent as you fall to the mat yourself). When practicing techniques, always start from a correct posture and a proper hold. Don't worry about what your opponents might do to you in the future; concentrate instead on mastering the techniques that will throw them to defeat. Though you should be familiar with all possible kinds of nagewaza, you will find it to your advantage to discover the one or two that particularly seem to suit you and work on them until you have mastered them completely.

1   2   3

7   8

Tewaza : Hand Techniques

TAI OTOSHI : body drop
Tai otoshi is a throwing method that involves your hands, hips, and legs working together to use the off-balanced condition of the opponent to throw him. The important point is timing. *Tai otoshi* is often used in contests because the physical size of the opponent is irrelevant. Even a small man can use it to throw a larger opponent.

1, 2. Stand in *migi shizentai* and push the opponent backward.

3, 4. When the opponent pushes back, use the force of his push to pull him forward. Timing is important here.

5. As you pull the opponent forward, turn around by pivoting on your right foot and bringing your left foot back.

6, 7. While the opponent is off-balance, place your right leg in front of his right leg. Make sure you place your right calf squarely across the opponent's right ankle.

8. Then throw the opponent forward in one motion.

4   5   6

POINTERS

Use of both hands: Get the opponent off-balance by pulling him forward. Turn the little-finger side of your left hand (which is the *hikite,* or pulling hand) out, pulling with your left arm while keeping the movement of your elbow in a horizontal plane. Push your right hand up, bringing your right forearm into position under the opponent's left armpit.

Use of the legs and hips: Relax your knees and see to it that they move into the opponent from a low position. The tips of the toes of the right foot are pointed in. Thrust up your chest so that your buttocks do not touch the opponent's body.

1   2   3

8   9   10

IPPON SEOI NAGE : one-arm shoulder throw

Ippon seoi nage uses the pushing power of the opponent to the maximum to throw him over your back and shoulder. Because the weights of you and the opponent are supported by your two feet and because it is much easier to throw the opponent when his center of gravity is high, this technique is the most effective one to use against a larger man. Very dynamic, *ippon seoi nage* is considered one of the most representative of judo throws.

1, 2, 3. From *migi shizentai,* push the opponent backward.

4, 5. When the opponent pushes back, take this opportunity to off-balance him to the right front corner.

6, 7. While pulling the opponent forward with your left hand, pivot on your right foot, turning your body to the left. Trap the opponent's right arm at the armpit with your right hand and lift him onto your back.

8, 9, 10. Straighten your knees and throw the opponent across your right shoulder and down in front of you.

26 Throwing Techniques

4　　　　　　　　5　　　　　　　　6　　　　　　　　7

POINTERS: Pull the opponent far enough forward to make him fully off-balance. Hold his right hand firmly against your chest. Curling your right little finger to the inside will thrust your chest up and bring your right arm in closer contact with the opponent's armpit. Before the throw, both knees must be fully bent, and your body's center of gravity should be over the tips of your toes.

1

2   *3*   *4*   *5*

1   *2*   *3*   *4*

1   *2*   *3*   *4*

6

FROM A RIGHT-HAND HOLD: You take a right-hand hold while the opponent has a left-hand hold. (This and other "fighting" holds are called *kenka yotsu.*) *Ippon seoi nage* is effective here. Push the opponent backward, and when he attempts to push back, use his reaction to throw him. Instantaneous speed is necessary to make this throw. The opponent loses his balance because you shift from right to left (photos *1-6*).

5

VARIATION 1

1, 2, 3. When your hip does not go in close in *ippon seoi nage,* or when the opponent moves to the right side, press against the area around his right knee with your right hand. The lower you press the more effective it will be since it will prevent him from advancing.

4, 5. Then throw the opponent as if you were sweeping his knee with your right hand.

This throw becomes most effective when the opponent is being cautious and withdraws his hips or stiffly stretches out his right hand.

5

VARIATION 2: This variation is used when your right *hikite* is not sufficiently effective.

1. You are attempting *ippon seoi nage* but the opponent suddenly turns backward to the left.

2. He steps forward and hooks his left foot on your left leg. Grab his right sleeve with your right hand while increasing the force of the pull of your left hand.

3, 4, 5. With your left hand, sweep off the left foot of the opponent which is hooked on your left leg and throw him over your shoulder.

Tobikomi   **1**   **2**   **3**

Hikidashi   **1**   **2**   **3**

MOROTE SEOI NAGE : two-arm shoulder throw

Morote seoi nage is in the same category as *ippon seoi nage* in that it uses the pushing power of the opponent to throw him completely over your shoulder. *Morote seoi nage* can be easily executed from a simple natural posture and is such a brilliant throw that it has become very popular today. One defect, however, is that the body weight of the opponent tends to concentrate excessively on your right elbow. Also, it is difficult to execute when the opponent holds you with his hands thrust out stiffly. It is common for people to start with *morote seoi nage* and then move on to *ippon seoi nage*.

TOBIKOMI (jumping in)

1, 2. From *hidari shizentai*, pivot on your left leg.

3, 4. Spin your left elbow into the opponent's left armpit; bend your knees and drop your hips and heave the opponent onto your back.

5, 6. Throw him over in front of you.

HIKIDASHI (pulling out): The *hikidashi* form of *morote seoi nage* is good for throwing large opponents because it makes it easy to get them off-balance.

1, 2. From *hidari shizentai*, take a big step backward with your right foot and pull the opponent close to you.

3, 4. Move your left foot back to your right foot and execute the throw.

4

POINTERS: Keep your left hand close in to the armpit of the opponent. To prevent injury to your elbow here, firmly grasp the opponent's jacket with the four fingers of your left hand.

3　　　　　　　　　　　　4　　　　　　　　　　　　5

8

KATA GURUMA : *shoulder whirl*

Kata guruma also uses the pushing power of the opponent as you lower your hips and grab his leg to heave him onto your shoulders and execute the throw. This is a very grand throw, but it sometimes happens that you are crushed by the weight of the opponent when he is not far enough off-balance.

1, 2. From *hidari shizentai,* draw the opponent well in with your left hand while withdrawing your left foot.

3, 4. Lower your hips and place the right side of your face onto the right thigh of the opponent as you grab his right leg.

5. Hoist the opponent onto your shoulders.

6, 7, 8. Then in one motion throw him in front of you to the left.

4

A MORE COMBAT-EFFECTIVE METHOD

1, 2. Swiftly kneel down on your right knee and take a low posture.

3, 4. Without lifting the opponent too high, throw him in one swift motion.

1

2

3

7

8

4   5   6

9   10

UKI OTOSHI : floating drop

Taking advantage of the pushing power of the opponent, *uki otoshi* uses *tai sabaki* to make the throw. *Uki otoshi*, because it involves difficult timing, requires the highest level of skill.

1, 2, 3. Push at the opponent from *migi shizentai*.

4, 5, 6, 7. When the opponent pushes back, keep your upper arms sealed tight to the side of your body and, with good timing, push upward as if to thrust into the opponent's armpit with your right forearm.

8, 9, 10. Pull your left *hikite* straight down and throw the opponent so that his falling movement causes him to spin in a half-circle on the ball of his own right foot.

Tewaza : Uki Otoshi   **35**

1   2

6   7

Koshiwaza : Hip Techniques

O-GOSHI : hip roll

O-goshi uses the pushing force of the opponent as you place your hip close to his body and then swing him around the hip to make the throw. It forms the basis of all hip techniques, and because *tai sabaki* here is relatively easy and the hips and legs are fully employed, it is a must for the beginner.

1, 2, 3. From *migi shizentai*, push the opponent backward.

4, 5, 6. When he pushes back at you, get him off-balance by pulling him with your left *hikite* to his right front corner. At the same time, pivot on your right foot to move your left foot in a backward arc to the front of the opponent's left foot.

7, 8, 9. Bend both knees and lower your hips as you bring your right hand way to the back of the opponent to grab hold of him. Pull the opponent in close to your hip and, as if lifting him from below, straighten your knees and throw him to the front with a twist of your hip.

36 Throwing Techniques

3   4   5

8   9

1   *2*   *3*

7   *8*

TSURIKOMI GOSHI : lifting-pull hip throw

Tsurikomi goshi enables you to use the pushing force of the opponent to lift him up onto your hips and throw him. It is a representative hip technique and is often used in contests because it can be executed directly from the natural posture at the same time that it makes full use of the feet and hips.

   1, 2, 3. Push the opponent backward from *migi shizentai*.

   4, 5. Utilize the force of the opponent when he pushes back and pull him with your left *hikite* to his right front corner to get him off-balance.

   6. Bring your left foot swiftly around to the front of the opponent's left foot as you thrust his left armpit up with your right arm.

   7, 8. Bend your knees and lower your hips to place your buttocks against the front of the opponent; heave him up and twist your hip to throw him to the front.

38 Throwing Techniques

4   5   6

POINTERS: Your right hand grasps the opponent's left collar. Bend your elbow and hoist him up as if to place your elbow in his left armpit.

Your hips move in from a low position. From behind your right armpit all the way along your back, your body should be in close contact with the opponent's.

1

2

6

7

SODE TSURIKOMI GOSHI : lifting-sleeve-pull hip throw

The times when you execute *sode tsurikomi goshi* are the same as for *tsurikomi goshi*. But here you hold onto the sleeve of the opponent to lift him up and throw him. This is an effective combat technique, and it is often executed to the right from a left hold and vice versa.

1. Stand in *hidari shizentai*. Hold the opponent's sleeve with your right hand.

2, 3. When the opponent, wary of a technique to the left side, shifts his center of gravity to the right front corner, take this chance to lift him up as you turn.

4, 5. Thrust your right *tsurite* (that is, your lifting hand) forward as you pull straight down with your left *hikite*.

6, 7. Throw the opponent to the front in one motion.

3   4   5

POINTERS: The two photos directly above show the arm positions for executing *sode tsurikomi goshi*. The right *tsurite* is thrust straight forward. It is acceptable here to cross the right *tsurite* and the left *hikite*.

1 2

5 6

HARAI GOSHI : hip sweep

In contrast to *o-goshi*, the hips here move in shallowly—the point of the hip bone is placed just below the opponent's navel and his body is held tightly against your side. You then twist your upper body to make the throw. This is a technique derived from *uki goshi* (a rising-hip throw; see p. 93). When the opponent pushes or goes around you, place your hips shallowly against him, bring his upper body close to yours, and sweep him with your leg. It is difficult to bring the opponent's body in close to yours, but with hard practice you will be able to perform this technique well.

HIKIDASHI (pulling out)

1, 2. From *migi shizentai,* push the opponent backward.

3, 4. Use his force when he pushes back at you to bring him off-balance to the right front corner.

3

4

7

8

5, 6. Pull the opponent's body close to your right side as you place your right leg along his thigh and knee.

7, 8. Twist your body to the left to sweep and throw the opponent.

1

2

3

MAWARIKOMI (spinning in): The main feature of this form of *harai goshi* is the way it effectively uses the opponent's psychology.

1, 2, 3. From a right hold, take your first step as if you were going to execute a technique to the left side so that the opponent shifts his center of gravity to the right. Take the chance he has given you by pivoting on the ball of your left foot and spinning back to the right.

4, 5, 6. Then sweep him to bring him down.

4

5

6

1

2

5

6

HANE GOSHI : hip spring

For *hane goshi* you half-bend your knee and spring into the opponent with your whole body to fling him down. This is a spectacular technique, because as soon as you have moved in on the opponent he will go flying high into the air.

1, 2. From *migi shizentai*, bring the opponent off-balance to the right front corner.

3, 4. While moving your left foot toward the front of the opponent's left foot, half-bend your right leg and place it across the opponent's right leg. Pull the opponent's body close to you and keep him in close contact until he is over you.

5, 6, 7, 8. Heave the opponent up high as you twist your hips to the left to throw him down in front and to the left.

46 Throwing Techniques

3

4

7

8

1

2

3

Ashiwaza : Leg Techniques

DEASHI BARAI : forward foot sweep
Here you sweep the opponent's foot in the direction it is advancing. The timing for this technique will not be right unless you use good *tai sabaki* to make the opponent advance his foot smoothly. When your timing is right, the opponent will fall down as if he had slipped.

   1, 2. Push the opponent from *migi shizentai.*

   3, 4. The instant the opponent advances with one foot, take a step back with your right foot and open your body to the right, thus drawing the opponent forward.

   5, 6, 7. With the sole of your left foot, sweep the anklebone of your opponent's right foot just before it touches the mat and pull straight down with your left hand to bring him down.

4

5

6 7

1

2

5

6

FROM KENKA YOTSU: *Deashi barai* can also be used when you are in *kenka yotsu*. The main feature here is that only the *tsurite* is used to make the throw. To ensure proper timing you must get the opponent to advance his foot smoothly (as shown in **2-6**). This is an effective combat technique often used in contests.

3

4

7

8

1 2 3

7 8

OKURI ASHI BARAI : assisting foot sweep

You can sweep the opponent down the moment he tries to move diagonally to the back. Because *okuri ashi barai* is largely a matter of timing, a small man can use it to topple a big man.

SIDE MOVEMENT

1, 2, 3. From *migi shizentai,* make the opponent move sideways to his left.

4, 5. At the moment the opponent is trying to move farther to the left, take a big step forward with your right foot.

6, 7, 8. With the sole of your left foot, sweep the anklebone of the opponent's right leg. As you do so, lift up the opponent with your right hand and pull down and in with your left hand to throw him down and along the direction he was trying to move in.

4   5   6

POINTER: The sweeping leg must not be bent but should be perfectly straight.

From a right hold   **1**   **2**   **3**

7   **8**

SASAE TSURIKOMI ASHI : supporting foot lifting-pull throw
The instant the opponent tries to move forward, you open your body ; then, propping your foot against his leg, you sway backward and twist your body to make the throw. *Sasae tsurikomi ashi* is often used because its movements are simple.

FROM A RIGHT HOLD

1. Hold the opponent from *migi shizentai.*

2, 3, 4. Advance your right foot to the side of the opponent's left foot and bring him off-balance to the right front corner.

5. Prop the sole of your left foot against the front of his shin slightly above his ankle and lean backward.

6, 7, 8. Twist your body backward to the left to throw the opponent.

FROM A LEFT HOLD : A person who uses left holds generally has a strong left foot. Consequently, the same technique can be executed from the left (*1-5*) without having to change the hold used above. Also this technique can be easily combined with other techniques. (See *o-soto gari* → *sasae tsurikomi ashi,* p. 167.)

4   5   6

From a left hold   1   2   3

4 5

Oikomi   *1*   *2*   *3*

Debana   *1*   *2*   *3*

KO-UCHI GARI : small inside clip

When the opponent moves forward, sideways, or backward, you move in to clip the inside of his right foot with your right foot (or his left foot with your left foot) to throw him. *Ko-uchi gari* can be combined with other techniques and is often used because it is hard for the opponent to countermaneuver you. (See *ko-uchi gari → morote seoi nage*, p. 156, and *o-uchi gari → ko-uchi gari*, p. 159.)

OIKOMI (dashing in)

1, 2, 3. Stand in *hidari shizentai.* The instant the opponent tries to retreat backward, jump forward.

4. With your left hand, thrust upward into the chin of the opponent ; with your right hand, squeeze and wring his left arm to the inside and push forward.

5, 6. At the same time, make the opponent fall by clipping his left heel with your left foot from the inside so as to draw his leg slightly outward and in the direction in which his toes were pointing.

DEBANA (thwarting the opponent)

1, 2. From *hidari shizentai*, push the opponent backward.

3, 4. When the opponent pushes back, open your body to the right.

5, 6, 7. Clip the left heel of the opponent from the inside with the sole of your left foot in the direction in which his foot was advancing. Squeeze and wring your right hand to the inside ; push the opponent down with your left hand.

4

5

6

4

5

6

7

Ko-uchi gari: side movement   **1**   **2**   **3**

SIDE MOVEMENT   **7**   Ko-uchi makikomi   **1**

1, 2. From *migi shizentai,* make the opponent move to his right side.

3, 4. Move half a step ahead of the opponent and, with the sole of your right foot, clip his right foot just after it has moved.

5, 6, 7. Squeeze and wring your left hand to the inside; push with your right hand on the opponent's left chest. Clip him so that his legs spread as he falls.

KO-UCHI MAKIKOMI : *small inner winding throw*

This is a form of *ko-uchi gari* (p. 56) in which you seem to roll into the opponent.

1, 2. With your right hand, forcefully draw the body of the opponent toward you.

3, 4. Step forward with your right foot and lower your body to move into the opponent's midsection. Then wrap your right arm around his right leg and start to topple him backward.

5, 6. Keep the back of your right shoulder tight against the chest of the opponent. As you fall and roll into him, knock the opponent down to the mat.

58   Throwing Techniques

4　　　　　　　　　　　　5　　　　　　　　　　　　6

2　　　　　　　　　　　　3

5

4

6

1   2   3

7   8

O-UCHI GARI : big inside clip

When the opponent moves forward, backward, or to the side, take the opportunity he offers you and clip the inside of his left leg with your right leg. Like *ko-uchi gari*, *o-uchi gari* is often used in contests because it is easy to combine with other techniques. (See *o-uchi gari → tai otoshi*, pp. 160, 161, and *o-uchi gari → ko-uchi gari*, p. 159.)

OIKOMI (dashing in)

1, 2, 3. From *migi shizentai*, move your left foot by *tsugi ashi* (see p. 16) so that it is behind your right foot.

4, 5. Pivoting on your left foot, turn the right half of your body to the opponent and draw him toward you. Then clip the inside of his left leg with your right leg so that he spreads his legs apart. Use your right hand to push on the neck of the opponent while your left *hikite* pulls toward the left side of your body.

6, 7, 8. Clip and throw the opponent backward to his left.

4 5 6

POINTERS: The tips of the toes of your right foot must be pointed when clipping the opponent. Sweeping the foot of the opponent directly sideways or upward will not be effective. If you pivot too much to the right, your face will turn to the side as you attempt to execute the clip and there is a chance that the opponent will countermaneuver you.

Debana   *1*   *2*   *3*

Ashi mochi   *1*   *2*   *3*

DEBANA   (thwarting the opponent)

1, 2. From *hidari shizentai,* make the opponent bring his right foot forward.

3, 4. Keeping your center of gravity low, draw the opponent's body to you and place your chest against his chest. Wrap your left foot around his right foot.

5, 6. While clipping the opponent, push with your own body to make him fall.

ASHI MOCHI   (leg grab)

1, 2. When the opponent grabs your inner lapel, move your head outside the hold by slipping it down and under his arm.

3, 4. Swiftly jump in close to the opponent and lift up his right leg with your left arm and draw it toward you.

5, 6, 7. While pushing the opponent with your body, clip his left leg with your right leg to topple him to the mat.

4

5

6

6

(rear view)

4

5

7

1

3

2

4

KO-SOTO GARI : small outside clip

Ko-soto gari uses your right foot to clip the outside of the opponent's left foot when he advances forward or retreats backward. It is very effective when the opponent has you in a non-standard hold.

DEBANA (thwarting the opponent)

1. The opponent tries to execute a technique from *kenka yotsu* and takes a big step forward with his left foot.

2. Draw his right arm well forward and bring him off-balance to his left back corner. At the same time, place your right leg along the outside of his right leg.

3, 4. Bring your right hand straight down as you lift up on the opponent as if to thrust your left forearm into his armpit. Sweep him with your right foot to topple him backward to the mat.

NIDAN BIKI (two-stage pull)

1, 2. From a *jigotai* slightly to the right, draw the opponent toward you and clip his left foot with your right foot.

3. When the technique is not effective and the opponent withdraws, take a step forward with your left foot. But do not loosen your hold on the opponent's hand that you pulled toward you.

4, 5, 6. Now loosen your hold a bit as you use your right foot to clip both of the opponent's legs.

1

2

6

7

O-SOTO GARI : *big outside clip*

The instant the opponent retreats or advances, bring him off-balance to the right back corner and clip his left leg with your left leg. *O-soto gari* is often used in contests and enables a small man to throw a big man.

1, 2. From *hidari shizentai,* advance your left foot toward the opponent.

3. When the opponent retreats, take a big step forward and place your right foot near the side of his left foot.

4, 5. With your right *hikite,* thrust down and toward the opponent's left side to off-balance him; keep your left *tsurite* well applied. Then place your chest up against the opponent's. As you do so, raise your left foot high in front of you.

6, 7. Making as if to plunge your head into the mat, swing your left leg backward and clip the opponent's left leg to bring him down.

3   4   5

(front view)

1

2

5

6

UCHIMATA : inner-thigh reaping throw

The instant the opponent advances, retreats, or turns around, bring him off-balance to the front; by inserting your leg between his legs and lifting with your leg at the inside of his right thigh, you can throw him to the mat. Because you have to stand on only one leg, it is rather difficult to maintain your balance, but *uchimata* is easily combined with other techniques and there are many who excel at it.

HIKIDASHI (pulling out)

1, 2. Push the opponent backward from *hidari shizentai*.

3, 4. When the opponent pushes back at you, use his force to bring your right foot to the side of your left foot as you pull him toward you.

5, 6, 7. Use the spring of your right leg and the lifting action of your left leg to help you lift up on the opponent's right inside thigh to throw him.

3

4

7

1

2

5

OIKOMI (dashing in)

1, 2. From *hidari shizentai*, push the opponent backward.

3, 4. As he retreats, put your right foot between the opponent's legs, well in under his thighs. At the same time, pull his body forward, making full use of your right *hikite* and left *tsurite*.

5, 6, 7. Employ your advancing force and the spring in your right foot to boost your left leg up into the right inside thigh of the opponent. Then twist in such a way that your body covers the opponent's as he goes down to the mat.

4

5

8

1   2   3

7   8

TAWARA GAESHI : *rice-bag reversal*

When the opponent tries to grab your leg, hoist up his body with both hands and heave him over your head as you fall back. *Tawara gaeshi* is a high-level technique requiring great skill and is often used as a method for getting into *katamewaza*.

1, 2. The opponent tries to grab your left leg.
3, 4. Encircle his upper body with both hands and start to hoist him up.
5, 6. Fall straight backward.
7, 8, 9. Throw him over your head.

4   5   6

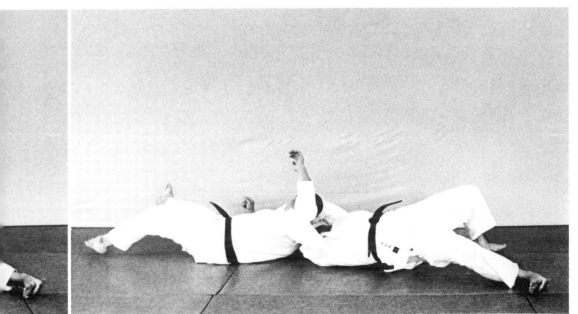

9

1   2   3

6   7

VARIATION

1, 2, 3. After struggling with you in the hold, the opponent grabs your belt from over your shoulder with his right hand.

4, 5, 6. Move your right arm around to the back of the opponent and place it over his neck.

7, 8, 9. Place your right foot between the opponent's legs and fall straight backward to bring him down. Keep your left arm wrapped around his right knee.

10, 11, 12. In a contest, it is common to apply *osaekomiwaza* immediately after the throw.

5

6

7

8

1 **2**

4 **5**

TANI OTOSHI : valley drop

There are various methods of *tani otoshi,* but fundamentally it is a technique in which you bring yourself close to the opponent's side and, falling down, throw him as if you were shoving him into a deep valley. It is one of the authors' favorite techniques and is often used to enter *katamewaza.*

METHOD 1

1, 2. When the opponent tries to execute *hidari uchimata,* grab his hips; while keeping your own hips low, thrust out your stomach and knock the opponent to the right side.

3. Move as if to clip both of the opponent's feet from behind with your right foot.

4, 5, 6. Fall forward to bring the opponent down to the right front corner.

84 Throwing Techniques

3

6

METHOD 2

1, 2. From *kenka yotsu,* try to execute *uchimata* (p. 68).

3, 4. But when the opponent sways backward, grasp this opportunity and move your left leg around behind and against the back of both of the opponent's legs.

5, 6. While your left hand is pulling down, thrust up with your right hand and fall onto your back to make the throw.

1

2

3

4

5

6

METHOD 3

1, 2. From *kenka yotsu*, grab the opponent's lapel from above his left arm with your right hand while your left hand holds his left sleeve near its mouth.

3, 4. Move so that you and the opponent are side by side in as much of a straight line as possible; with your right hand, take hold of the back of his left thigh while swinging your right leg around behind him.

5, 6. As you fall backward, scoop up the opponent's leg to bring him down.

Yoko Sutemiwaza : Tani Otoshi **87**

1   2   3

5   6

HIKIKOMI GAESHI : *back-fall reversal*

As in *obitori gaeshi* (p. 80), grab the opponent's belt from over his shoulder and fall sideways to make the throw. This is a technique which is often used to enter *katamewaza*.

METHOD 1

1. With your right *hikite* pull the opponent's left sleeve to the side.

2, 3. As the opponent reacts by trying to recapture his balance, pull his left arm close in to the right side of your body; at the same time, grab his belt from over his shoulder with your left hand and draw him toward you.

4, 5, 6. The opponent will try to move backward.

7, 8, 9. Take advantage of the opponent's motion and, almost placing your left ear along his left side, revolve sideways.

10, 11. You should apply *osaekomiwaza* immediately.

4

7

8

9

10 11

2

3

1

METHOD 2

1. From *kenka yotsu,* grab the opponent's left sleeve near its mouth with your left hand.

2, 3, 4. Break the grip of your opponent's left *tsurite* by pulling down with your left hand and pushing down and in with your right hand at the top of the wrist. Then, with your right hand, grab his back from over his shoulder and draw him toward you sideways.

5, 6. Step forward onto your left foot and insert it between the opponent's legs as you raise your right foot up against his right inner thigh.

7, 8, 9. Drop your body sideways to throw the opponent.

10, 11. Then immediately apply *osaekomiwaza.*

4

5

6

7

8

9

10 11

Sumi otoshi

Sukui nage

Morote gari

Koshi guruma

Uki goshi

Other Nagewaza

SUMI OTOSHI : corner drop
Bring the opponent off-balance to the left back corner and throw him with good timing. This technique is also call *kuki nage* (the air throw).

SUKUI NAGE : scoop throw
When the opponent attempts *uchimata,* insert your hand between his legs from behind and throw him in a scooping motion.

MOROTE GARI : two-arm clip
Move into the opponent's chest and clip his legs to make the throw.

KOSHI GURUMA : hip whirl
Hold the opponent on your back with one arm held tightly around his neck and use your hips like the axle of a wheel to throw him.

Ushiro goshi

Utsuri goshi

O-tsuri goshi   Ko-tsuri goshi

UKI GOSHI : rising hip throw
Place one hand on the opponent's belt from under his armpits; let your hip enter shallowly, pull him tightly against you, and twist your upper body to make the throw.

USHIRO GOSHI : rear hip throw
When the opponent attacks with a hip technique, counter by lowering your center of gravity below his; then lift his hip up with your own hips to make the throw.

UTSURI GOSHI : hip shift
When the opponent attacks with a hip technique, draw him to you and shift your hips to throw him.

O-TSURI GOSHI : big lifting hip throw
Grab the opponent's belt from over his shoulder; throw him as in *o-goshi* (p. 36).

KO-TSURI GOSHI : small lifting hip throw
Grab the opponent's belt from under his armpit and throw him as in *o-goshi*.

Ko-soto gake

Harai tsurikomi ashi

O-guruma

Ashi guruma

Hiza guruma

O-soto guruma

KO-SOTO GAKE : small outside hook

Start with *ko-soto gari* (p. 64) ; then place the clipping foot on the mat and throw the opponent over your knee by using the forward motion of your upper body.

O-GURUMA : big whirl

Get the opponent off-balance as you did for *harai goshi* (p. 42) and throw him around your thigh.

HIZA GURUMA : knee whirl

Bring the opponent off-balance to the front corner. Place the sole of your foot on the opponent's knee and throw him with your upper body.

HARAI TSURIKOMI ASHI : pulling-lift leg sweep

Pull and lift the opponent's upper body as you sweep his right leg at the ankle with your left foot to make the throw.

ASHI GURUMA : leg whirl

Put your right calf on the opponent's right knee and throw him over and around it.

O-SOTO GURUMA : big outside whirl

Get the opponent off-balance as you did for *o-soto gari* (p. 66). Then, with your right leg, sweep both his feet to make the throw.

Sumi gaeshi

Ura nage

Yoko otoshi

Yoko gake

SUMI GAESHI : corner reversal
From a defensive posture *(jigotai)*, place your right instep on the opponent's left inner thigh and throw him by pulling him to you and rolling backward.

URA NAGE : rear throw
When the opponent attempts *o-soto gari* or some hip technique, draw him toward you, drop your hips lower than his, and fall straight backward to make the throw.

YOKO OTOSHI : side drop
Slip your left leg to the outside of the opponent's right foot and fall sideways to make the throw.

YOKO GAKE : side hook
Use both hands to off-balance the opponent to the side. Then place your left foot on the back of his right foot and bring him down by falling sideways.

Soto makikomi

Hane makikomi

Yoko wakare

Yoko guruma

SOTO MAKIKOMI : *outside wrap-around throw*
Off-balance the opponent as in *harai goshi* (p. 42) and thrust your right arm across his shoulder as you spin to the right and wrap him around you to make the throw.

HANE MAKIKOMI : *springing wrap-around throw*
Start as in *hane goshi* (p. 46) and then thrust your right arm over the opponent's shoulder as in *soto makikomi* to make the throw.

YOKO WAKARE : *side split*
Bring the opponent off-balance to the front and, sticking your right foot out to his right side, fall backward to bring him down.

YOKO GURUMA : *side whirl*
When the opponent attempts *uchimata* or some hip technique, draw him to you and, placing your right foot between his legs, fall while turning to make the throw.

3

Grappling
Techniques

Sutemiwaza, *a fall, an unsuccessful throw, or a partially successful throw will often leave both competitors on the mat to grapple until one or another achieves victory. Grappling techniques are called* katamewaza *(or* newaza*), and there are several types. In the case of* osaekomiwaza *(mat holds), victory can be achieved by maintaining complete control over the opponent for a specified period of time. For* shimewaza *(strangle holds) and* kansetsuwaza *(armlocks), victory is achieved when the opponent passes out or the pain forces him to submit (he says* Maitta, *"I give up," or taps his opponent's body or the mat with his hand or foot more than two times). Grappling techniques are neither as flashy nor as brilliant as the* nagewaza *presented in chapter 2, but they have an inner depth that can contribute to the improvement of all your techniques. A well-rounded approach to judo that combines lots of practice, throwing, and grappling on the mat reaches to the very essence of the sport.*

You are on your back

The opponent is on his back

The opponent is on all fours

You are on all fours

Basic Postures and the Attack Pattern

When you are on your back
- Take a position in which you can roll around easily by curling up your body.
- Grasp the opponent's lapel and bring his head lower than his hips.
- Use your feet and legs to hook and grab as if they were your hands and arms.

When the opponent is on his back
- Take a position in which you can turn around easily.
- Keep your head above your hips when you attack.
- When you are not in control of one or both of your opponent's legs, do not thrust your hand farther than his belt.
- Do not move your feet in such a way that the insteps touch the mat. Keep your toes up so that you can move quickly and with good traction.

When the opponent is on all fours
- Place your chest in close contact with the opponent's back.
- Although there are times when you attack from the opponent's head, it is more effective to attack from his side or rear.

When you are on all fours
- Since it is difficult for you to attack from this position you should avoid taking it as much as possible.
- If you unavoidably find yourself in this position, try to direct your head toward the opponent so that he cannot get behind you.

Kesa gatame

Kuzure kesa gatame

Osaekomiwaza : Holding Techniques

KESA GATAME : sash hold

In *kesa gatame*, the opponent is lying face up on the mat. From his side, pin him down from shoulder to armpit, in the form of a diagonal sash. Hold the opponent's left arm deep in your right underarm. Place your left hand around the back of the opponents' neck from over his right shoulder. Use your forearm to raise and restrain his neck. Grasp the sleeve of the opponent's left arm with your right hand and forcefully draw his hand to the right side of your stomach. Place your left leg under the opponent's left shoulder. Bend your right leg and open it to the rear.

Two important points are to keep your body in close contact with the opponent and to keep the opponent's left arm trapped tightly in your underarm. Maintain a position in which you will be able to coordinate your moves with your opponent's.

There is a modification of this hold called *kuzure kesa gatame*. Its shape and the way both legs are opened are both quite similar to those of *kesa gatame* except for the use of the left hand. Here you slip your left hand under the opponent's right armpit and grab the back of his collar. Depending on the opponent's movements, you may release your hand and place it on the mat to keep him under control.

If you are being held in *kesa gatame* or *kuzure kesa gatame*, you can escape in either of the following ways : (1) Twist your body to the left and hook your right leg on the opponent's right foot ; then, with your right hand, grab the opponent's belt from the back, pull him close to your body, and turn him over to the left side. (2) Pull in your left shoulder and twist your body to the left to release the opponent's hold on your left arm ; then turn onto your stomach to extricate yourself.

ATTACK 1 (from above)

1. Hold both of the opponent's knees to check their movement.

2, 3. Pin down the opponent's left inner thigh with your left knee to further restrain the movement of the leg. Lift up the opponent's left collar with your left hand and draw his left sleeve toward you with your right hand.

4, 5. Keeping your chest in close contact with your opponent's, hold his left arm firmly with your right hand and apply the hold.

100 Grappling Techniques

ATTACK 2 (from above)

1. With your left hand, reach under the opponent's right armpit and grasp his left lapel.

2. Press down with your chest and with your right hand grasp his left sleeve.

3, 4. Open your left arm to the right and turn the opponent's body over while pulling his left arm out and into you.

5, 6. When the opponent turns over, move in to apply the hold.

ATTACK 3 (from below)

1, 2. With your left hand, grasp the opponent's left lapel near his neck. Trap the opponent's left arm under your right upper arm and slip your right hand through to grab his right lapel and draw him toward you.

3, 4. With your left hand grasp the opponent's belt on his right side; using the push of both of your legs and the pull of both of your arms, draw the opponent toward you to straighten out his body.

5, 6, 7. With your right foot, kick the opponent's left leg and raise your left foot up against his right leg to make him turn over.

8, 9, 10. Apply the hold as soon as the opponent is on his back.

4　　　　　　　　　　　5

Kata gatame

KATA GATAME : shoulder hold

The opponent is lying face up on the mat. You are on his right side. While you lower your upper body, press down on the opponent's right arm and head with your own right arm and head to control them. Stretch your left foot out straight; bend your right arm and keep it in close contact with the opponent's body. Then clasp both of your hands under him, palms together in the shape of a cross.

You have to be careful to lower your head straight down when you hold the opponent in order to prevent him from turning and disentangling himself. *Kata gatame* combines holding techniques and strangle techniques, and if it is well executed the hold on the neck of the opponent will become tighter as he tries to escape by rolling over. You must completely control the opponent's right arm.

To get out of this hold, clasp both of your hands and press the opponent's neck with your right elbow in order to create space between you and him ; then turn your body over to the left or right to make your escape.

Kami shiho gatame

Kuzure kami shiho gatame

KAMI SHIHO GATAME : upper four-corner hold

The opponent is lying on his back. Approach him from his head. Pass both of your hands beneath his arms ; then grab both sides of his belt and draw him toward you. Clamp down tightly with your arms and slightly raise your upper body. Press your body down on the opponent's face and chest to hold him. For forceful restraint, keep your chest close to the opponent's and lay your chin on his solar plexus.

When the opponent tries to wriggle free, spread your legs into a straddle position and let them act as a stabilizer. It is important to keep your body and your opponent's body in a straight line. Keep your elbows off the mat.

KUZURE KAMI SHIHO GATAME : modified upper four-corner hold

In *kami shiho gatame,* you execute the hold with your body and the opponent's body in one straight line. But in *kuzure kami shiho gatame,* your bodies form a shallow V. As the opponent lies on his back, cover his right shoulder and the right side of his neck with your body. Pass your right hand over his right shoulder and around his arm and grasp his belt at the back. Then slip your left arm between his left arm and the mat and get a strong hold on his belt in back. Clamp down tightly with both arms and straighten your upper body. Spread both of your legs wide apart and hold the opponent by pressing your chest on his.

If you make your body too rigid when executing the hold your opponent will soon escape. Put power only into the vital areas and ride atop the opponent with your body relaxed. Keep your body and the opponent's in the shape of a shallow V.

There are two methods of getting out of *kuzure kami shiho gatame:* (1) Insert your left hand between you and the opponent and create a greater space by moving your body up and down. Press up with your left hand and pull down with your right hand. As you do this, make a small half-turn to the right and lie prone on the mat. (2) Grasp the opponent's back belt from over his shoulder with your left hand. With your right hand grab the opponent's belt in front and twist your body to bring you and him into a straight line. While twisting, raise up your right hand suddenly and pull with your left hand to disengage yourself from the hold.

1

2

3

4

5

6

ATTACK 1 (from above)

1. Grab the opponent's belt in front with your right hand and with your left hand grab his right knee to control its movement.

2. Press down on his right inner thigh with your right knee to further restrain him.

3. Grasp the right lapel of the opponent with your left hand; then grab his left lapel with your right hand and pull him toward you.

4. With your left hand, reach over and around the opponent's left shoulder and grab his belt in the back.

5, 6. Place your chest close to the opponent's to complete the hold.

ATTACK 2 (from above)

1. Grab the opponent's belt at the sides from under his legs.

2, 3. Keep your chest in close contact with the body of the opponent and raise him up to restrain his movement.

4, 5. Grasp his left sleeve with your right hand and pull it toward you.

6, 7, 8. With your body held close to the opponent's, shift him around on the mat to make the hold.

1   2   3

4   5   6

7   8   9

ATTACK 3 (from above)

1. Grasp the opponent's right lapel after thrusting your left hand under his left armpit.

2, 3. Turn over your left wrist and place your left knee on the right side of and next to the opponent's head.

4, 5. With your left knee as a pivot, use both hands to turn the opponent over.

6, 7. When the opponent is about to turn over, thrust your right hand below his left armpit and pull your body close to his.

8, 9. When the opponent has turned over, pounce on him to make the hold.

1

2

(rear view)

ATTACK 4 (from above)

1. Control the opponent's body with your chest and get a shallow grip on his right lapel with your right hand.

2. When you attempt to strangle him with your left hand, the opponent will tighten his left arm and bunch himself up.

3, 4. Take this opportunity to press down the opponent's left shoulder with your left hand and open your body to the right. At the same time, use your right hand to roll the opponent's body around your left hand diagonally to his left.

5, 6. When the opponent has rolled over, apply the hold at once.

3

4

5

6

1 2 3

6 7

8 9

ATTACK 5

1, 2. With your left hand, take a deep hold on the opponent's left lapel; with your right hand, grab his left arm from below.

3, 4. Now use your left hand to grab the opponent's belt in back from across his shoulder and pull his body closer to you.

5, 6, 7. Thrust your left leg between the opponent's legs and with your left foot kick up into the opponent's right inner thigh to make him roll over.

8, 9. As soon as the opponent is on his back, apply the hold.

FOUR WAYS TO CONTROL THE OPPONENT'S UPPER BODY

A. Grasp the opponent's belt in back from over his left shoulder with your left hand and place your head in his left armpit to control his movement.

B. Pass your left arm under the opponent's head and grab his left lapel from under his left armpit; pull your chest close to his.

C. With your left hand, grab your own left lapel from over the opponent's head and pull it down to control him.

D. When the opponent grabs his belt, thrust your left arm over his left shoulder and then under his arm to grab and half-wrap his belt (or jacket, *D'*) over his wrist.

4   5

A   B

C   D

D'

B

YOKO SHIHO GATAME : side four-corner hold

Yoko shiho gatame is author Inokuma's favorite holding technique. There are two
ways to apply it.

A. As the opponent lies on his back, hold him under your body at a right angle.
Go around his shoulder and grab his belt with your left hand. Place your right hand
between his legs to prevent him from escaping. Spread both your legs apart but
keep the right leg bent and close to the opponent's body. The most important thing
is how you use your left arm. The little finger of the left hand, which is grasping
the opponent's belt, should be turned upward; the left arm should be held tight
around the opponent. Do not place your body too far over the opponent. But do
thrust your left chest forward to make the hold more effective.

B. As the opponent lies on his back, hold him under your body at a right angle.
Pass your right hand between the opponent's legs and grab his belt in back. Slip
your left hand under his head and grip the left side of his collar, keeping your body
close to his. This hold uses your entire body and controls the opponent by focusing
on his hips. The use of both legs is the same as in **A**, above. Release techniques
are the same as in *kuzure kami shiho gatame* (p. 104).

ATTACK 1 (from above)

1. Control the opponent by holding both of his knees with both of your hands.

2. Straighten out the opponent's knee and lean over his left leg.

3, 4, 5. Scoop up the opponent's left side and pass your left hand over his shoulder to grab his belt at the back.

6, 7, 8. Using your right hand, pull your entangled right leg free and apply the hold.

ATTACK 2 (from above)

1, 2. From between the opponent's legs, grab the tail of his jacket with your right hand. With your left hand, grasp his knee and, while controlling his hips, step over his right leg.

3. Keep your chest close to the opponent's body and with your left hand grab his collar from under his head.

4. Then apply the hold.

4

ATTACK 3 (from below)

1. Hold the opponent's arms with both of your hands.

2, 3. Keep your chest close to the opponent's body and turn him around by pulling him with both hands.

4. Apply the hold.

4

ATTACK 4 (from above)

1. Press down on the opponent's right shoulder with your right knee to restrain the movement of his upper body. With your right hand, grasp his left sleeve, and with your left hand, grab his left knee.

2, 3. Use both of your hands to heave up the opponent and turn him. Simultaneously control the opponent's body with your left knee.

4. Apply the hold.

4

ATTACK 5 (from above)

1, 2. Grasp the opponent's belt in back with your left hand. With your right arm, hold his right side to control his upper body. Then hook his left arm with your right from under his armpit.

3. While keeping your upper body close to the opponent's upper body, pull him forward with both hands and roll him on the mat using his left hand as a lever.

4. Apply the hold while still in control of the opponent's upper body.

4

1

2

4

5

8

ATTACK 6 (from below)

1, 2. With your right hand, grab the opponent's right collar, and with your left hand, hold his inner thigh and push him forward.

3, 4, 5, 6. The instant the opponent tries to rise, grasp his belt in back with your left hand to pull him over.

7, 8. Use your right arm, neck, and head to control the opponent's right leg while you keep your body close to his.

9, 10. While still in close bodily contact with the opponent, apply the hold.

116 Grappling Techniques

3

6

7

9

10

ATTACK 7 (from below)

1. The opponent grabs your belt in the back and, with his left hand slipped under your right arm, tries to turn you over.

2. Bring your left knee up and clamp down with your right arm. Your neck should be under the left side of the opponent's body.

3. Get a strong grip on the opponent's left sleeve with your right hand and slip your right foot in front of the opponent's right foot.

4, 5. Raise your neck well up; push up on the opponent's inner thigh with your left hand to turn him over.

6, 7, 8. When you have turned the opponent over, apply the hold at once while your body is still in close contact with his.

118 Grappling Techniques

ATTACK 8 (from below)

1. Hold the opponent's right leg with both of your arms.

2, 3, 4. Topple the opponent by bending his right leg inward. As he falls, grab his belt in the back or the tail of his jacket from between his legs and pull your body into close contact with his.

5, 6. Apply the hold while still in close bodily contact with the opponent.

Osaekomiwaza : Yoko Shiho Gatame **119**

1

2

3

4

(side view)   *(rear view)*

EXTRICATING YOUR LEG

When trying to apply a holding technique it often happens that, even though you are in good control of the opponent's upper body, your feet get entangled and trapped in his legs. You must be able to get your feet out deftly without jeopardizing your control of the opponent. There are several ways of doing this, and six of these are presented here.

METHOD 1

1. Control the opponent's upper body and, with your right hand, grasp his left knee.

2, 3, 4. Raise the opponent's leg with your right hand to control his movement. Slip your left knee under his hip. This will cause the hip to rise and, at the same time, his leg lock to loosen. You will then find it easy to extricate your right leg.

METHOD 2

1, 2. Hold the opponent's left side to control his upper body.

3, 4, 5, 6. While shifting your upper body forward, use your left foot as if executing *tate shiho gatame* (p. 126) to release your right leg.

3', 4', 5' (variation). From **2**, grab the opponent's knee from inside with your right hand. Loosen the opponent's right leg by using your right hand and left leg. Then extricate your leg as if entering *yoko shiho gatame* (p. 112).

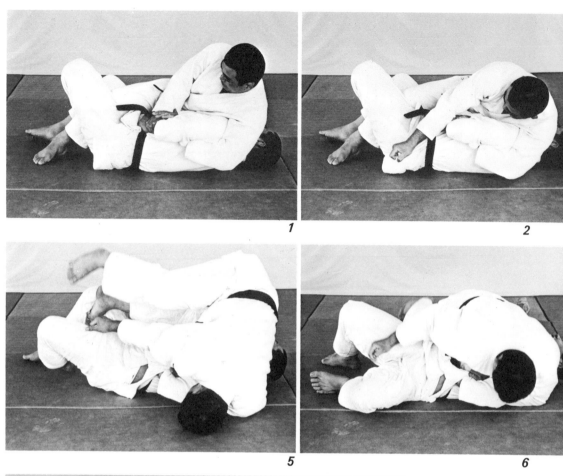

1

2

5

6

7

METHOD 3

1, 2, 3. Control the opponent's upper body by using his belt or his jacket flap to tie down his left arm at the wrist.

4, 5. Use your right hand and left foot to loosen the opponent's leg lock and extricate your leg as in *tate shiho gatame* (p. 126).

6, 7. Then apply *yoko shiho gatame* (p. 112).

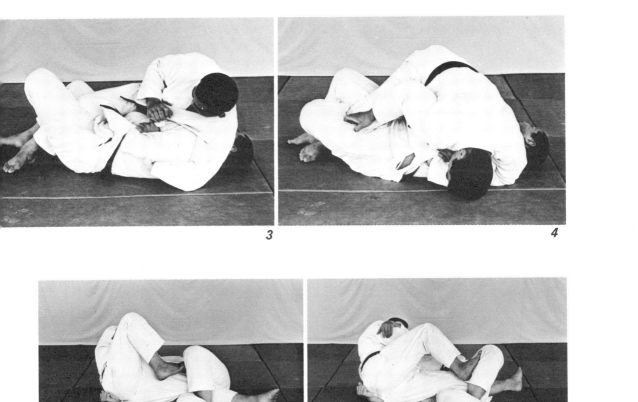

3   4

1   2

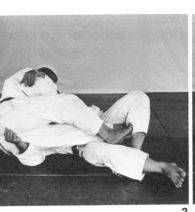

3   4   5

METHOD 4

1, 2. Control the opponent's upper body and hold the left side of his body in your armpit. Use your right foot to loosen his leg lock.

3, 4. Pull your hips well out and use your right foot to release your leg. Be careful not to let the opponent turn you over here.

5. When you have pulled out your left leg, twist your hips and reverse positions with the opponent. Keep your body close to his.

1

2

6

7

8

9

10

METHOD 5: *niju garami* (double entanglement)

1. Both of your legs are trapped by the opponent.

2. Lower your hips and draw up your right foot as far as you can.

3. Then powerfully thrust out and straighten your right leg.

4, 5, 6. 7. If the above doesn't break the entanglement, raise your right knee from the floor and, while shifting your foot, slide your right heel close to the opponent's hip. This will make it impossible for him to entangle your legs.

8. Use your right hand to slide the opponent's left leg lower.

9, 10. While controlling the opponent's upper body, keep your body close to his and use your left foot to extricate your leg.

3

4

5

1

2

3

METHOD 6: *niju garami* (double entanglement)

1. Both of your legs are trapped by the opponent.

2. Press down on the opponent's right foot with your left foot and break the entanglement by bending your right leg upward.

3. Turn your raised right leg in a circle to the outside and place your knee on the mat. Bring your heel near the opponent's hips.

A

1

2

B

1

2

TATE SHIHO GATAME : straight four-corner hold

Your whole body is astride the opponent, and if you cannot control him completely there is a chance that you will be turned over. But a small man well trained in this technique can use it to handle a large man. There are several ways of holding the opponent's upper body in this situation. Two are presented here.

A. With your right hand, grasp the opponent's belt in back from over his shoulder; with your left arm, scoop up his right armpit to keep his body close to yours.

B. Encircle the opponent's neck with your right arm and grab your own belt on the right side. Encircle the opponent's right arm with your left arm and grasp your own left collar to control his upper body. Photo **2** shows how to use your legs, but, depending on the opponent's movements, there are times when both legs become entangled.

To extricate yourself from this hold, swing both of your legs widely to the right and left and move your hips; then with your free hand break the opponent's hold. You can also loosen the hold by raising your knee and wriggling the hand which is under the opponent's control.

126 Grappling Techniques

1

2

3

4

ATTACK 1 (from above)

1. With your left hand, hold the opponent's right leg from below and grab the tail of his jacket. With your right hand, grab near his knee to control the movements of his right leg. Then lift your leg over his left leg.

2, 3, 4. With your right hand, grasp the opponent's belt in the back from over his shoulder; with your left hand, scoop up the left side of his body.

5. While controlling the opponent's upper body, slide your body upward to apply the hold.

ATTACK 2 (from above)

1, 2. Go behind the opponent and, with both of your hands, grab his lapels from under his armpits to control his movements.

3, 4. Draw your right hand toward you and, with your left arm, wrap the opponent's left arm and slide your body upward and over. It is important to use both of your feet effectively here.

5. Apply the hold.

128   Grappling Techniques

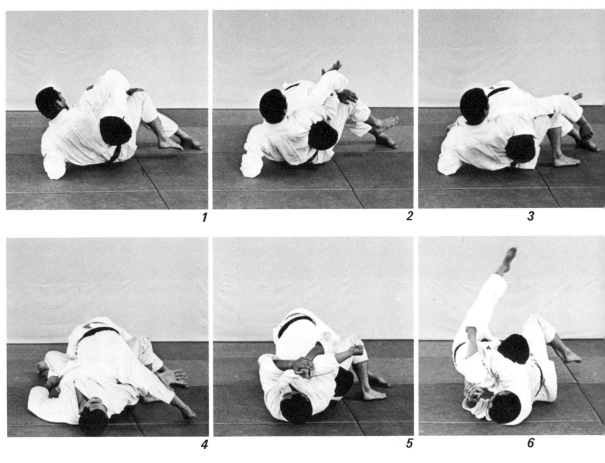

1   2   3

4   5   6

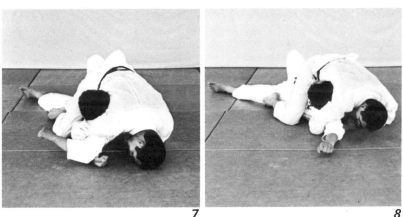

7   8

ATTACK 3 (from below)

1, 2. With your right hand, grasp the opponent's belt in back from over his head to bring him off-balance.

3, 4. When the opponent tries to regain his balance by thrusting out his left arm, reach over his head and capture his arm from below with your right arm.

5, 6. Control the opponent's captured left arm with both of your hands and use your feet deftly to roll him over.

7, 8. Then swiftly apply the hold.

*A more effective
okuri eri jime*

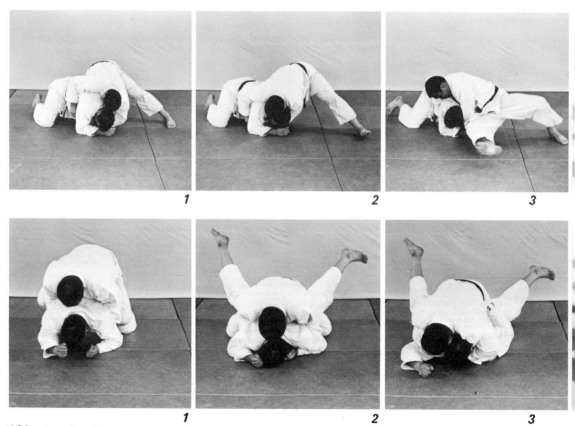

1   *2*   *3*

1   *2*   *3*

Shimewaza : Strangle Techniques

OKURI ERI JIME : collar strangle

Approach the opponent from behind and, sliding your right hand under his right armpit, grip his left lapel. With your left hand, get a strong grip on the opponent's right collar from under his chin. Then press your head against the back of the opponent's head while you pull your right hand downward. Draw your left hand toward the lower left side of your body to strangle him.

This strangle hold will be more effective if you use both of your legs to restrain the opponent's legs and prevent him from moving about on the mat.

ATTACK 1 (from the front)

1, 2. With your right hand, get a shallow grip on the opponent's right collar from under his right armpit. Stay in close to the opponent and control his movements with your chest. Slip your left hand in from under the opponent's left ear and get a deep grip on his right collar.

3, 4. Crush down on the opponent's body to place all your body weight on him. Apply the strangle hold.

4

ATTACK 2 (from the rear)

1. Get astride the opponent and grip his collar from under both sides of his body with both of your hands ; keep your body close to his.

2. Put both of your legs between the opponent's thighs from the inside and crush down on his body.

3. With the body of the opponent flattened, pass your left hand under his chin and get a deep grip on his right collar.

4. Apply the strangle hold while still in close bodily contact with the opponent.

4

HADAKA JIME : naked strangle

Kneel on your left knee behind the opponent and pass your right hand and arm over his right shoulder and across the front of his throat. Be sure that the part of your forearm just above the wrist is against the opponent's throat. Then tightly clasp both of your hands above his left shoulder. Shift back slightly to pull the opponent toward you and apply the strangle hold.

1   2

3   4   5

ATTACK (from above)

1, 2, 3. Get astride the opponent; when he tries to lie on his stomach, push on both of his elbows to crush him down.

4, 5. As the opponent falls forward and then reacts by trying to heave up back-ward, apply the strangle hold.

KATAHA JIME : single-wing strangle

Get behind the opponent as in *okuri eri jime* (p. 131) and use your right hand to grip his left collar firmly from under his chin. Slide your left arm (which is reaching through from under the opponent's left armpit) upward to control the opponent's left arm. Then apply your left arm at the nape of the opponent's neck to execute the strangle hold. The important point here is to raise the opponent's left hand high up behind him before thrusting forward to strangle him.

1 **2**

3 **4** **5**

ATTACK (from above)

1. Get astride the opponent and control his body with both of your legs. Stay in close to the opponent and grab his left collar with your left hand from under his left armpit. With your right hand grab the left collar from under his chin as in *okuri eri jime* (but not as deep).

2, 3. Revolve to the left, thrusting your left hand up behind the opponent's head.

4, 5. Use both of your legs effectively to control the opponent's body and, thrusting your left hand farther in, apply the strangle hold.

Nami juji gatame

Gyaku juji gatame

Kata juji gatame

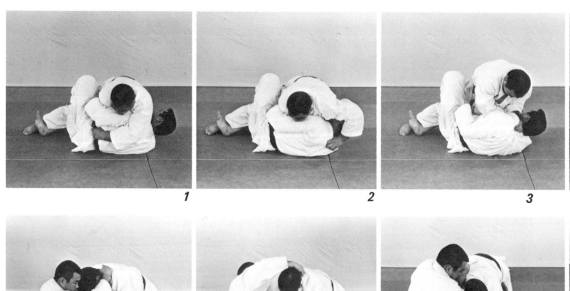

1　　　　**2**　　　　**3**

1　　　　**2**　　　　**3**

KATA JUJI JIME : half cross strangle

The opponent is lying on his back. Straddle him and, while controlling his body with both of your legs, grab his left collar with your left hand; hold the small-finger side of that hand toward the left side of the opponent's body. Cross your right arm over your left arm and, with your right hand, get a deep grip on the opponent's right collar; hold the palm of your hand upward. Pull on both hands swiftly and, while placing your full weight on the opponent's body, strangle him.

Gyaku juji jime is a cross-lock like *kata juji jime* but with the palms of both hands held upward. In *nami juji jime*, both hands should enter deep into the opponent's jacket with the little-finger sides touching his neck. The choking action for both of these holds is the same as for *kata juji jime*.

ATTACK 1 (from above)

1. Relax your hold on the opponent's body slightly; thrust your right hand in from the base of his chest and grab his right collar with the palm of your hand facing upward. At this time you may also feint *osae-komiwaza*.

2. With your left hand, grab the opponent's left inner collar with the thumb inside and fingers out.

3, 4. Cross both hands and apply the strangle hold.

4

ATTACK 2 (from below)

1. Grasp the opponent's left collar with your left hand; with your right hand, grab his back collar on the left and pull him toward you.

2. Take advantage of the opponent's forward motion and shift your body to the left as you cross both of your arms by slipping your right hand over the opponent's head. (Keep hold of the opponent's jacket as you do this.)

3, 4. Pull the opponent to your chest with both hands and with your right foot trap his right knee to control his body; then execute the strangle hold.

4

Yoko sankaku jime

Ura sankaku jime

1

2

3

4

5

6

7

YOKO SANKAKU JIME ATTACK 1 (from above)

1. The opponent is on all fours. Grab his belt at the back with your left hand and with your right hand, grasp his back collar and pull him forward and down.

2. When the opponent opens his right elbow and thrusts out his arm in an effort to regain his balance, take this opportunity to wedge your left heel into his right armpit. With your right hand, grasp his left sleeve.

3, 4. Rolling to the left, lock the opponent's right arm and neck with both legs.

5. Control the opponent's left arm by wrapping it with his belt or jacket.

6, 7. With your right hand, pull the opponent's right arm and then lock your legs in a triangle to apply the hold. Each of your ankles should be at a right angle.

SANKAKU JIME : triangular strangle

Sankaku jime is a locking technique in which you lock your opponent's neck and arm by forming a triangle with the top of the ankle of one leg in the hollow of the knee of the other leg. Among *katamewaza,* it requires the very highest level of technique, and it can only be executed effectively when you are able to use your legs as deftly as your hands. Because the opponent is strangled by your legs, the power of this hold is quite impressive.

There are several strangling methods for *sankaku jime.* Here we shall introduce three that are representative.

Yoko sankaku jime (side triangular strangle) : The opponent's neck and arm are caught in both of your legs from the side.

Ura sankaku jime (rear triangular strangle) : The opponent is lying on his back. You are at his head and trap his neck and arm.

Omote sankaku jime (front triangular strangle) : You hold the opponent's arm and neck from below.

Omote sankaku jime

1   **2**   **3**

4   **5**   **6**

YOKO SANKAKU JIME ATTACK 2 (from above)

1. The opponent is on all fours. With your left hand, grasp his belt at the back and with your right hand, grab his right collar from under his left armpit.

2. When you try to turn the opponent over to the left, he will try to thwart you by placing his right elbow on the mat. Take this opportunity to thrust your left heel into his right armpit.

3, 4. Rolling to the left, lock the opponent's right arm and neck with your legs.

5. Control the opponent's left arm with his belt or jacket.

6. Pull the opponent's right arm toward you with your right hand and lock your legs triangularly to strangle him. Each of your ankles should be bent at a right angle.

URA SANKAKU JIME ATTACK (from above)

1. Straddle the opponent, who is on all fours, and get control of him by grabbing his collar with both of your hands from under his armpits.

2, 3, 4. Revolve to the left and feint *okuri eri jime* (p. 131).

5, 6. Thrust your right foot far in from under the opponent's right shoulder and with both of your hands pull his right hand toward you to control it.

7. Place your left leg along the left side of the opponent's neck from over his shoulder. Fix your left leg in the hollow of your right knee. Both of your ankles should be bent at a right angle.

8. Then hold both knees close together to apply the strangle hold.

OMOTE SANKAKU JIME ATTACK (from below)

1, 2. Place the inside of your right knee against the opponent's left neck. With your right hand, pull your opponent's right arm as far as possible to your right side.

3, 4. Bend your right ankle at a right angle, and raise it up, locking it with your left knee. Now fix your left ankle in a right angle.

5. Twist your hips to the left and strangle the opponent with your legs. If the lock isn't effective, pull up your right shin with your left hand.

Shimewaza : Sankaku Jime **139**

From the inside

From the outside

Kansetsuwaza : Armlock Techniques

UDE GARAMI : entangled-arm armlock

Ude garami is a lock in which, while holding the opponent's wrist with your right hand, you grasp your own right wrist with your left hand and twist his arm backward at the elbow. Your body should be crossed over the opponent's. The opponent's left arm should be bent almost 90°. Apply downward pressure on both of your wrists and pull the opponent toward you with both hands. To make the lock more effective, press down firmly on the opponent's body and fix it so that he cannot move his left shoulder. There are two methods of applying this lock, from the inside and the outside.

1   *2*   *3*

ATTACK 1 (from above)

  1. Start to control the opponent's upper body from above.

  2. When the opponent carelessly thrusts out his left hand, grab his left wrist with your right hand. Push your left hand in from under the opponent's left arm and grip your own right wrist with it.

  3. Pull the opponent's wrist toward you with your right hand to apply the lock.

1   2   3

4   5   6

ATTACK 2 (from above)

1. Insert your left hand under the opponent's left armpit and grab his left wrist.

2. Keeping in close bodily contact with the opponent, press down on him to the right front (press along the diagonal formed by the opponent's right shoulder and left hip).

3, 4. Place your right hand on your left hand and pull out the opponent's left arm.

5, 6. Open your body to the right and, laying your left elbow on the opponent's left upper arm, push up on his left wrist with both of your hands to apply the lock.

1   2   3

ATTACK 3 (from below)

1. With your left hand, grip the opponent's left inner collar and draw him toward you. When he tries to regain his balance and places his left hand on your knee or on the mat, grasp this opportunity to grab his right wrist with your right hand.

2. Thrust your left hand under his armpit and grab your own right wrist.

3. Push upward with your right hand to apply the lock.

Kansetsuwaza : Ude Garami   **141**

(side view)

(rear view)

UDE HISHIGI JUJI GATAME : arm-taking cross armlock
Ude hishigi juji gatame (or just juji gatame) is a technique in which you are over the opponent so that your bodies form a "cross." Hold the opponent's right wrist with both hands and then pull his right arm straight out as you clamp your knees around it. Your body should be at a right angle to your opponent's. The lock will be more effective if it is applied with the opponent's right thumb upward. By slightly spreading both of your legs, it will be easier for you to lock the opponent's right arm firmly with both of your thighs. If you place your buttocks far in on the opponent's right shoulder, the shoulder will become fixed and immobile.

142 Grappling Techniques

1   2   3

4   5

6   7

ATTACK 1 (from above)

1. Straddle the opponent. Grab the front of his left sleeve with your right hand from under his right armpit. With your left hand, grasp the front of his left sleeve from over his left shoulder.

2, 3. Move forward, pulling on both of the opponent's arms. As you move, hook your right foot onto the outside of his left thigh across his abdomen.

4, 5, 6. While rolling the opponent over, turn your body at a right angle to his; pull his left arm well toward you and keep your hips in close to his body.

7. Hold the opponent's right arm with your left hand and raise up your stomach slightly to apply the lock.

Kansetsuwaza : Ude Hishigi Juji Gatame   **143**

Attack 2   *1*   *2*   *3*

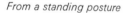

From a standing posture   *1*   *2*   *3*

ATTACK 2 (from below)

1. From below, grab the opponent's right arm with your left hand; then, with your right hand, take his right inner collar and pull him toward you.

2, 3. Form the cross by raising your hips, bringing your left leg around to the left side of his neck. (You may also form the cross by grabbing the opponent's left ankle from the inside with your right hand.)

4, 5, 6. Thrust up both of your legs, stick out your stomach, and bring your legs down to execute the lock.

FROM A STANDING POSITION

1, 2, 3. From *migi shizentai,* swing up your right foot and plant it firmly in the opponent's right armpit.

4, 5. At the same time, kick up your left foot and form the cross with the opponent.

6, 7, 8. Lock the opponent's right arm firmly between your knees and, while lowering your legs, pull the opponent over and around and apply the lock.

4

5

6

4

5

6

7 8

From a kneeling posture

From below

1

2

3

4

UDE HISHIGI UDE GATAME : *arm-taking armlock*

Ude hishigi ude gatame is a technique in which, having straightened out the opponent's arm and fixed his wrist on your right shoulder, you place both of your hands on the outside of his elbow and press down to apply the lock. The important point is that you swiftly grab the opponent's arm as he thrusts it out. If you bring both of your hands a bit down from the upper part of the opponent's arm to his elbow, the technique will be more effective.

ATTACK (from a standing position)

1, 2. When the opponent thrusts out his right arm from *hidari jigotai,* open your body to the left and thrust in to drive the elbow of your right arm toward the opponent's left side.

3, 4. Place your right hand on the opponent's left elbow and your left hand over your right hand. Pull the opponent down to the front and apply the lock.

1　　　　　　　　　　**2**　　　　　　　　　　**3**

4　　　　　　　　　　**5**

UDE HISHIGI HIZA GATAME : *arm-taking knee armlock*

Ude hishigi hiza gatame is a technique in which, having straightened out the opponent's left arm and fixed his wrist on your right upper arm, you place both of your hands on the outside of the opponent's left elbow and, with your right knee on his left collarbone, press down to apply the lock. There is another method in which you hold the opponent's left arm to the right side of your body and, placing your right knee on his left collarbone, press down to apply the lock.

ATTACK (from below)

1. With your left hand, grab the opponent's left collar and draw him toward you.

2. When he resists by placing his left hand on your knee or on the mat, move your right hand under his left arm and place it on his left elbow from the outside.

3. Place your left hand over your right hand and trap the opponent's left arm with the upper part of your right arm; with your left foot push and straighten out the opponent's right leg. While bringing the opponent down, straighten out his left arm.

4, 5. Press on his left collarbone with your right knee and apply the lock.

1 *2*

3 *4* *5*

UDE HISHIGI WAKI GATAME : arm-taking side armlock

Here you trap the opponent's left arm firmly in your right armpit and stretch the arm out while twisting it backward at the elbow. The little finger of the opponent's left hand should be facing upward if the lock is to be effective. Do not hold the left arm too far in. Use your right elbow to fix the opponent's left elbow from above and raise your wrist to apply the lock.

ATTACK 1 (from above)

1, 2. At the moment the opponent is on all fours, thrust your right hand in from the top and under his left side near his shoulder.

3, 4. Sweep the opponent's left arm to the side with your right forearm and trap it in your left armpit.

5. Tighten your armpit and fall on the opponent to apply the lock.

148 Grappling Techniques

ATTACK 2 (from below)

1. The opponent tries to cover you and thrust his right hand under the left side of your body.

2. Grab the opponent's right knee with your right hand and tighten up your left arm just above his elbow to trap his right arm.

3, 4. Stick your head out behind the opponent's right side; open your body to the left and, with the back of your head, crush down on his body to apply the lock.

A

B

1

2

3

4

5

UDE HISHIGI HARA GATAME : arm-taking stomach armlock

Here you take the opponent's right wrist with your right hand, fix it on the lower part of your stomach, and, having grabbed the opponent's right collar with your left hand to control his neck, apply the lock (**A**).

Another method is to tie up the opponent's right arm with your right leg and, placing your left leg on the right, fall on the opponent to straighten out his right arm and apply the lock (**B**).

ATTACK (from above)

1. Attack from above with *okuri eri jime* (p. 131).

2. When the opponent tries to stand, capture his right arm with your right leg.

3. Keeping in close to the opponent, pull out his right arm while pressing down on his body. Keep your right leg above your left as you hold the opponent's arm.

4, 5. Change the position of your legs (right foot below and left foot above) and, with your body still close to the opponent's, twist your left hip to apply the lock.

4

Combination
Techniques

In an actual contest you will not always be able to defeat the opponent with a single technique. If your technique is unsuccessful and you have nothing else to try, the opponent may be able to counter and defeat you with a technique of his own. Thus you must prepare techniques that you can use in combination with each other to create various types of attack possibilities. These combination techniques are called renrakuwaza, *and what they demand is speed and good timing. Daily practice in them is necessary so that, during a contest, you will be able to switch your tactics fluidly in a split second. Often, a split second is all the time you will have.*

1   2   3

5   6

Nagewaza → Nagewaza

YOUR OWN TECHNIQUE TO YOUR OWN TECHNIQUE

Shifting from one technique to another technique is commonly called *saki no saki*. You apply one technique to get the opponent off-balance and then another technique to throw him. This very positive combat strategy is called *kake kuzushi*. The numbers in the headings below tell you on what page in this book the techniques combined are explained in detail.

Ippon seoi nage → ko-uchi gari (26, 56)

1, 2, 3, 4. Attempt *migi ippon seoi nage.* The opponent resists by sticking out his belly and swaying backward.

5, 6. While bringing your body back to its former position, place your right leg against the opponent's right leg and control the leg with your right hand.

7, 8. With your right shoulder, push the opponent along his right chest and shoulder, and then roll forward.

9, 10. Roll so that the opponent's right shoulder is completely down on the mat.

4

7

8

9 10

Ko-uchi gari → morote seoi nage (56, 30)

1, 2, 3. From *hidari shizentai,* push the opponent and attempt *hidari ko-uchi gari.*

4, 5. The opponent stretches out his left foot and pushes back in an attempt to regain his balance.

6, 7. With good timing, bend your knee completely and execute *hidari seoi nage.*

8, 9. Use leg-strength to throw the opponent forward in one motion.

156 Combination Techniques

4

5

8 9

O-uchi gari → morote seoi nage (60, 30)

1, 2, 3. From *hidari shizentai,* push the opponent and attempt *hidari o-uchi gari.*

4, 5. The opponent drops his right foot back and pushes at you in an attempt to regain his balance.

6. Take this chance to completely bend your knee and execute *morote seoi nage.*

7, 8. Use the strength in your legs to throw the opponent forward in one motion.

O-uchi gari → ko-uchi gari (60, 56)

1, 2, 3. From *hidari shizentai,* push the opponent and attempt *hidari o-uchi gari.*

4, 5. When the opponent eases up on his right foot and tries to step farther back, continue advancing in *tsugi ashi* and attempt *hidari ko-uchi gari.*

6, 7. Twist and pull your right hand tightly toward the inside, and with your left hand push the opponent on the chin to knock him backward. It is important here to topple the opponent by using your left foot more to push his left leg open than to clip it.

O-uchi gari → tai otoshi 1 (60, 24)

1, 2, 3. From *migi shizentai,* push the opponent and attempt *migi o-uchi gari.*

4, 5. He eases up on his left foot and pushes back in order to regain his balance.

6. Take this opportunity to get the opponent off-balance to his right front corner ; pivot around and in on your right foot. Then, keeping your posture low, take a step forward and place your right foot in front of the opponent's right foot.

7, 8. As you turn your body, straighten out both of your legs and throw the opponent forward with *tai otoshi.*

160 Combination Techniques

O-uchi gari → tai otoshi 2 (60, 24)

1, 2, 3. From *migi shizentai,* push the opponent forward and attempt *o-uchi gari.*

4, 5. When the opponent reacts by shifting his center of gravity to the right, take this opportunity to remove your right leg which made the clip. Take a step forward and stretch your right leg in front of the opponent's body.

6, 7. Swiftly bring the opponent off-balance to the front and, using your *hikite* and *tsurite* effectively, throw him forward with *tai otoshi.*

O-uchi gari → o-soto gari (60, 66)

1, 2, 3. From *hidari shizentai* push the opponent and attempt *hidari o-uchi gari.*

4, 5. When the opponent eases up on his right foot and tries to step farther back, take a big step forward and place your right foot next to his right foot.

6, 7. Lower your right hand and raise your left hand to bring your body close to the opponent's. At the same time, take a big step forward with your left foot.

8. Use the back-pedaling motion of the opponent to help you clip him down with one stroke of your leg in *o-soto gari.*

O-uchi gari → uchimata (60, 68)

1, 2. From *hidari shizentai*, draw your opponent to you and attempt *hidari o-uchi gari*.

3, 4, 5. When the opponent lifts his right foot to thwart your move, pull him forward and jump in at him.

6, 7. Spring up and swiftly twist your body to throw the opponent. When the technique does not work at first, you must sometimes repeat it again and again (called *ken ken uchimata*).

1

3

2

O-soto gari → harai goshi (66, 42)

1, 2, 3. From *migi shizentai,* push the opponent and attempt *o-soto gari.*

4. The opponent pulls his right foot back and leans forward to resist your move.

5, 6. Pivot on the tips of your left toes to open your body to the left and pull the opponent toward you. Here, make effective use of your *tsurite* when you pull the opponent so that his head leans to the right.

7, 8. While sweeping up the opponent's right leg with your right leg, twist your body to throw him in one motion with *harai goshi.*

5

4

6

7

8

1

2

3

4

5

6

7

O-soto gari → sasae tsurikomi ashi (66, 54)

1, 2. From *hidari shizentai,* step forward with your right foot and attempt *o-soto gari.*

3. The opponent tries to resist by placing his center of gravity over his right foot.

4, 5. Take this chance to draw your left hand in while you lift the side of the opponent with your right hand to enter *sasae tsurikomi ashi.*

6, 7. Sway back and twist your body to make the throw.

1   2   3

7   8

Tai otoshi → o-uchi gari → tai otoshi (24, 60)

1, 2, 3. From *migi shizentai,* pull the opponent toward you and attempt *tai otoshi.*

4, 5, 6. When the opponent successfully resists you, switch to *o-uchi gari.*

7, 8, 9. The opponent eases up on his left foot and comes forward to regain his balance.

10, 11, 12, 13. Take this opportunity to execute *tai otoshi* in one motion.

In order to execute one technique after another, good timing and speed are of course necessary. But one must also have great stamina. The above is a high-level technique which is very effective in contests and which can be mastered only by constant practice.

4

5

6

9

10

11

12 13

1   2   3

7   8

O-uchi gari → tai otoshi → sasae tsurikomi ashi (60, 24, 54)

1, 2, 3. From *hidari shizentai,* push your opponent and attempt *o-uchi gari.*

4, 5, 6. Take the opportunity presented you when the opponent eases up on his right foot and attempt *hidari tai otoshi.*

7, 8, 9. The opponent leaps across your left leg to thwart your *tai otoshi* and then brings his center of gravity over his right foot in order to regain his balance.

10, 11, 12, 13. Take this opportunity to execute *sasae tsurikomi ashi.*

Here, three techniques are combined. But it is possible to combine more than three techniques. Practice so that you will be able to execute your best techniques one after the other.

4 5 6

9 10

11 12 13

1　　　　　　　　2　　　　　　　　3

4　　　　　　　　5　　　　　　　　6

7　　　　　　　　8

YOUR OPPONENT'S TECHNIQUE TO YOUR OWN TECHNIQUE

Taking your opponent's technique and turning it into your own technique is commonly called *ato no saki*. Here you use the power of the opponent's technique against him to make the throw. Relying only on this strategy, however, will not help your own techniques improve in the long run.

Koshiwaza → utsuri goshi (38, 36, 93)

1, 2. From *migi shizentai,* the opponent attempts a hip technique, either *tsurikomi goshi* or *o-goshi.*

3. Lower your hips and resist the opponent's move.

4, 5. Stick out your stomach and lift the opponent. Use the motion of the return of the opponent's body to the ground to shift his hips to your left hip.

6, 7, 8. Draw in the opponent fully and twist your hips to throw him with *utsuri goshi.*

O-soto gari → ura nage (66, 95)

1, 2, 3. From *migi shizentai,* the opponent takes a big step forward and attempts *migi o-soto gari.*

4. Spread your right leg to lower your hips, then hug the opponent and pull him toward you.

5, 6. Fall back and throw the opponent straight back in one motion.

O-uchi gari → o-uchi gaeshi (60)

O-uchi gaeshi is the name given to the technique used to counter the opponent's *o-uchi gari*.

1. From *kenka yotsu*, the opponent attempts *migi o-uchi gari*.

2, 3. Lean backward and thrust your left foot forward. Here, concentrate your power in the tips of your toes and keep your left leg perfectly straight.

4, 5. Twist your hips to throw the opponent.

174 Combination Techniques

1 **2** **3** **4**

5 **6** **7**

Uchimata → sukui nage (68, 92)

1, 2. When the opponent attempts to execute *migi uchimata,* thrust your right hand out and at the same time insert your left hand between his legs.

3, 4. Lean back swiftly and lift the opponent's body to the front.

5. When the opponent's body is about to come down, take a half-step forward with your right foot and, while flinging up the opponent with your right hand, place his body on your left hip.

6, 7. Twist your hip to throw the opponent with *sukui nage* while keeping your body close to his.

O-uchi gari → morote seoi nage (60, 30)

1, 2, 3. From *hidari shizentai* the opponent attempts *hidari o-uchi gari.*

4. Take two steps forward and remove your trapped right foot.

5, 6. Pivot and swing your left leg around until your feet are together; utilizing the force of the opponent's push, enter *seoi nage.*

7, 8. Throw the opponent in one motion.

176 Combination Techniques

Uchimata → tai otoshi (68, 24)

1, 2. From *kenka yotsu,* the opponent attempts *migi uchimata.* It is important here that you thrust your right hand into the opponent's armpit to make sure that you are not drawn in by him.

3. Take a low posture and bring your left foot to your right foot.

4. Take a step slightly forward with your left foot and place your left foot in front of the opponent's left foot.

5, 6, 7. Use the opponent's momentum to help you bring him down.

1   2   3

7

Nagewaza → Katamewaza

In a contest *nagewaza* alone might not be enough for a winning score (*ippon*), and there are often cases in which you have to try to win by using *katamewaza* as well. Be prepared for this and practice daily to master moving from throwing techniques to grappling techniques.

YOUR OWN TECHNIQUE TO YOUR OWN TECHNIQUE

Ippon seoi nage → yoko shiho gatame (26, 112)

1, 2. You attempt *migi ippon seoi nage*.

3, 4, 5. You get off-balance and your *hikite* is not effective. Drop to your right knee and throw the opponent down.

6, 7. Keep your chest close to the opponent while holding onto his right arm.

8, 9. Step in close to the opponent and apply *yoko shiho gatame*.

4

5

6

8

9

O-uchi gari → kesa gatame (60, 99)

1, 2, 3, 4. From *hidari shizentai,* push the opponent and throw him with *o-uchi gari.*

5, 6. Do not relax your right *hikite* as you use the momentum of the throw to approach the opponent from his left side.

7. Clamp down on the opponent's left arm and, keeping his left side close to your body, apply *kesa gatame.*

Sasae tsurikomi ashi → kuzure kami shiho gatame (54, 104)

1, 2, 3. Throw the opponent with *sasae tsurikomi ashi*.

4, 5. Do not loosen your grip with your left hand but swiftly fall on the opponent and place your chest in close contact with his body.

6, 7. With your left hand, grab the opponent's belt from over his shoulder and apply *kuzure kami shiho gatame*.

Tomoe nage → ude hishigi juji gatame 1 (72, 142)

1, 2. Attempt *hidari tomoe nage*.

3. When it isn't effective, do not loosen your left *hikite* but pivot on your right leg and twist your hips so that your body and the opponent's body are perpendicular, forming a cross.

4, 5. Place your left leg across the opponent's neck and, jutting out your stomach, bring your leg down.

6. Then apply *juji gatame*.

Tomoe nage → ude hishigi juji gatame 2 (72, 142)

1, 2, 3. Attempt *tomoe-nage.*

4, 5. When it isn't effective and the opponent topples forward, lift your left leg twist your hips, and thrust your left leg under his chin.

6. Apply *juji gatame* while face down on the mat.

1

2

3

5

6

Tai otoshi → ude hishigi juji gatame (24, 142)

1, 2, 3, 4. Execute *hidari tai otoshi.*

5, 6. Without loosening your *hikite,* lift it up and clamp down on your opponent's left arm with both of your legs to form the cross.

7, 8. Pull your knees together and, fixing the opponent's left arm, apply *juji ga-tame.*

184 Combination Techniques

4

7

8

1

2

3

4

5

YOUR OPPONENT'S TECHNIQUE TO YOUR OWN TECHNIQUE

Ippon seoi nage → okuri eri jime 1 (26, 131)

1. The opponent attempts *migi ippon seoi nage.*

2, 3. Go a half-step around the opponent on your right foot and get him off-balance to thwart his *seoi nage*

4, 5. Squeezing with your right arm, crush down on the opponent's body and move forward to place your body weight over your right hand to apply *okuri eri jime.*

1

2

3

4

5

6

7

8

9

Ippon seoi nage → okuri eri jime 2 (26, 131)

1. The opponent attempts *migi ippon seoi nage.*

2, 3. Take a half-step forward with your right foot to counter the opponent.

4. Bring your right hand, which is holding the opponent's collar, back around his neck as you shift your body to the left side.

5, 6, 7. While keeping your body in close contact with the opponent's, grab his left inner thigh with your left hand and roll him over onto his right side.

8, 9. The roll will make the opponent's collar, held by your right hand, close in on his neck and give a better strangle hold.

1 2 3

5 6

Uchimata → tani otoshi → yoko shiho gatame (68, 84, 112)

1, 2. The opponent attempts *migi uchimata.*

3. Lower your hips to resist.

4, 5. Push the opponent forward in an attempt to crush him.

6, 7, 8. When the opponent tries to stand up and regain his balance, thrust out your left foot and execute *tani otoshi.*

9, 10, 11, 12. Get on top; then apply *yoko shiho gatame.*

This is one of Yasuhiro Yamashita's favorite combination techniques.

4

7

8

9

10

11 12

1

4

2

5

3

Katamewaza → Katamewaza

Combination techniques involving throws are performed instantaneously. *Katame-waza* combination techniques lack this speed, but for this reason allow you to map out a strategy involving holds, chokes, and locks in a variety of combinations. Of course the instant you actually move from one technique to another you will have to be quick and agile. Work out your own combinations and practice them until you have mastered them.

YOUR OWN TECHNIQUE TO YOUR OWN TECHNIQUE

Kesa gatame → ude hishigi waki gatame (99, 148)

   1. Hold the opponent down in *kesa gatame.*

   2, 3. The opponent tries to escape by drawing in his right elbow and rolling onto his stomach.

   4, 5. While staying close to the opponent, hold his left arm under your right arm and apply *waki gatame.*

Kesa gatame → yoko shiho gatame (99, 112)

1. Hold the opponent down in *kesa gatame.*

2, 3. The opponent pulls on his left elbow and with his right hand removes your arm from around his head in order to escape.

4, 5. Hold the opponent's right arm while keeping his body close to yours.

6, 7. While holding the opponent's right arm, switch to *yoko shiho gatame.*

Kesa gatame → okuri eri jime (99, 131)

1. Hold the opponent down in *kesa gatame*.

2, 3. The opponent loosens his right arm and, wriggling his shoulders, tries to escape by turning face down.

4. Grab the opponent's right collar with your left hand while still close in on him. (Your hand must move in from under the opponent's chin.)

5, 6. Put all your body weight on the opponent and apply *okuri eri jime.*

Okuri eri jime → kuzure kami shiho gatame (131, 104)

1. Thrust your right hand in under the opponent's underarm. With your left hand, attack with *okuri eri jime*.

2, 3. When the opponent tries to pull your left arm with his left hand and moves his arm away from his body, take this opportunity to trap his arm by thrusting your left arm under his armpit from over his shoulder. Keep your head in close contact with the opponent and, using both of your legs, deftly work down his body.

4. Still holding his arm, get on top and apply *kuzure kami shiho gatame*.

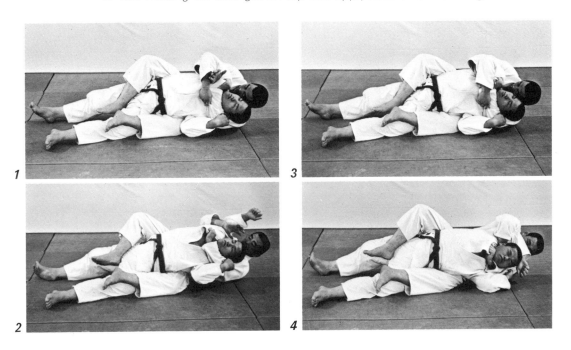

Okuri eri jime → kataha jime (131, 133)

1. Approach the opponent from his back and attempt to apply *okuri eri jime*.

2, 3. Look for a chance to move your right hand behind the opponent's neck to control his right arm.

4. Thrust your left hand well under the opponent's chin and apply *kataha jime*.

Katamewaza (yours) → Katamewaza **193**

Kuzure kami shiho gatame → ude hishigi juji gatame (104, 142)

1. Hold the opponent down in *kuzure kami shiho gatame.*

2, 3. The opponent tries to escape by turning face down.

4. The instant you enter *juji gatame* your hips are in close contact with the opponent's body. Hold his right arm and, lowering your hips as much as possible, turn to make your body perpendicular to his in the form of a cross.

5, 6. Close your elbows tight and, holding the opponent's arm, apply *juji gatame.*

Kesa gatame → ude hishigi juji gatame (99, 142)

1. Enter *kesa gatame*.

2, 3. The opponent relaxes his right hand and tries to extricate himself by using his shoulder and rolling over.

4, 5. Grab the opponent's right arm with your right hand while still in close to him and turn your body so that it crosses over his.

6, 7. Place your knees together and hold the opponent's right arm to apply *juji gatame*.

Tate shiho gatame → ude hishigi juji gatame 1 (126, 142)

1. Enter *tate shiho gatame*.

2, 3. The opponent wriggles his hips and tries to escape by pushing upward with his right hand.

4, 5. Grab his right arm with your left hand. While balancing yourself with your right hand, turn to cross over the opponent at the moment he is trying to roll over.

6. Apply *juji gatame*.

Detail showing use of the elbow

Tate shiho gatame → ude hishigi juji gatame 2 (126, 142)

1. Enter *tate shiho gatame.* Here, grab the opponent's right arm as in *kesa gatame* (p. 99) and grip your own belt with your left hand.

2, 3. Purposely let the opponent escape so that he ends up on all fours.

4, 5. Then form a cross with him and pull in your elbow to apply *juji gatame.*

Kuzure kami shiho gatame → yoko sankaku jime (104, 136)

1. Control the opponent's upper body and attempt *kuzure kami shiho gatame.*

2. The opponent resists and starts to go on all fours by using his shoulder.

3. As soon as the opponent is on all fours, hook the right side of his body with your left sole; you are still in control of his upper body.

4, 5. Clamp both of your legs over the opponent's right arm and head and turn him over to the left side.

6, 7. Bind up the opponent's left arm with his jacket or belt to control his upper body.

8. Form a triangle with your legs and apply *yoko sankaku jime.*

Yoko sankaku jime → kuzure kami shiho gatame

Yoko sankaku jime
→ jigoku jime   **1**   **2**   **3**

Yoko sankaku jime → kansetsuwaza   **1**   **2**

Yoko sankaku jime → kuzure kami shiho gatame (136, 104)

1, 2. Your *yoko sankaku jime* is not effective. When the opponent tries to wriggle out, place your right hand on the mat to prevent his escape.

3. Move on top of the opponent's upper body.

4. Disentangle your legs to apply *kuzure kami shiho gatame*.

Yoko sankaku jime → jigoku jime (136)

Jigoku jime (hell strangle) is a variation of *yoko sankaku jime*.

1. Your *yoko sankaku jime* is not very effective.

2. Thrust your right hand between your legs; grip the opponent's right lapel.

3. Pull his lapel with your right hand as you entwine your legs tightly in a triangle. The strangling action results from the actions of your hands and feet.

Yoko sankaku jime → kansetsuwaza (136)

1. Your *yoko sankaku jime* is not very effective.

2. Grab the opponent's right wrist with your right hand and slide your right outer thigh in the direction of the elbow to lock it.

Sankaku garami → okuri eri jime (131)

1. The opponent attacks you by trying to hold your left leg with his right arm.

2. Push the left side of his neck with your left hand and turn him aside. At the same time, swing your right foot up.

3. Shift your hips swiftly and swing your right foot down to the front.

4. Straighten out both of your feet to crush down on the opponent. Here, grab hold of the opponent's trousers or belt to prevent him from rolling over.

5. Lock your legs in a triangle to apply *sankaku garami* (triangular entanglement); keep close to the opponent and attack his elbow.

6. When he resists, apply *okuri eri jime;* maintain the lock with your legs.

1

2

3

4

5

Ude garami → kuzure kami shiho gatame (140, 104)

1. 2. When you attack the left arm of the opponent with *ude garami,* he grabs his belt.

3, 4. Wind the opponent's jacket or belt over his left arm.

5. Then apply *kuzure kami shiho gatame* while keeping your body close to the opponent's.

Ude hishigi ude gatame → tate shiho gatame (146,126)

1, 2. From below, draw the opponent down to you and attack with *ude gatame*.

3. The opponent tries to escape by turning over.

4, 5. Take this opportunity to control his upper body and switch to *tate shiho gatame*.

Ude hishigi hara gatame → jigoku jime (150)

1, 2. Attack the opponent's right arm with *hara gatame.*

3, 4. When the opponent tries to stand up, keep his arm trapped between your legs and roll forward over his back. As you roll, hold the opponent's left arm from under his armpit with your left hand.

5, 6. Grasp the opponent's left collar with your right hand and apply *jigoku jime.*

YOUR OPPONENT'S TECHNIQUE TO YOUR OWN TECHNIQUE

Yoko shiho gatame → kuzure kami shiho gatame (112, 104)

1, 2. When the opponent has you in *yoko shiho gatame,* grab his belt from over his shoulder with your left hand; thrust your right elbow into your side to get your hand under his stomach. Now grab his inner thigh. Bunch your feet up so that they can be thrust into the opponent's chest.

3, 4. Making use of the opponent's attempt to move back, throw him over your head so that, when he lands, your body and his lie in a straight line.

5, 6. After the opponent is on his back, immediately go into *kuzure kami shiho gatame.* Throwing the opponent like this is commonly called *teppo gaeshi* and is done by those with powerful arms. But if your opponent is well trained, it may be difficult to execute this technique.

1

2

3

4

5

6

Yoko shiho gatame → yoko sankaku jime (112, 136)

1, 2. When the opponent controls your leg from above and tries to apply *yoko shiho gatame,* push the left side of his head with your left hand.

3, 4, 5. Wrap your legs to form a triangle around the opponent's head and right arm.

6. Pull the opponent toward you and apply *yoko sankaku jime* from below.

Okuri eri jime → kesa gatame (131, 99)

1. The opponent attacks with *okuri eri jime* while you are on all fours.

2. When the opponent slips his right hand rather far in under your right armpit, thrust out your right leg and quickly turn your right hip downward.

3, 4. Roll over. While so doing, keep your right arm closed tight to control the opponent's right arm. As soon as you are around on the mat, hold the trunk of the opponent's body with your left hand.

5. Then apply *ushiro kesa gatame* (*kesa gatame* from the rear).

206 Combination Techniques

Kuzure kami shiho gatame → okuri eri jime (104, 131)

1. The opponent attacks from above.

2, 3. As he tries to control your upper body, wrap your left arm around his neck and grip his left lapel.

4, 5. Intentionally allow the opponent to control your upper body and apply *kuzure kami shiho gatame.*

6. Thrust your right hand under the opponent's right armpit and grab the back of his jacket.

7. Pull with both of your hands and strangle the opponent by raising your stomach.

5

Training

Judo is a sport that uses practically every part of your body. Judo training centers on randori *(free practice), and during such training you naturally develop the strength that judo requires. But today's judo also demands that you build up overall strength and the various parts of your body in a more deliberate way to lay a powerful foundation that will support your judo techniques. In this chapter we shall look at some of the training methods you can use, and especially at weight training.*

About Training

For judo, you must work to develop your muscles, stamina, flexibility, power, and speed, and strive to develop all-around body strength. Power and stamina particularly are essential in contests; the competitor who has trained harder to develop them will in the end emerge the victor.

There are many ways to build up your strength, such as weight training, isometric training, interval training, circuit training, and so on. You may also gain some benefit from engaging in sports such as soccer and basketball. This chapter presents a variety of methods, but focuses on weight training, which involves lifting heavy objects like barbells and dumbbells. Weight training is a good choice for judoists because it is specifically designed to develop the strong muscles they need.

But physical training is a means, not an end in itself. Such training is meaningless if it is not directly tied in to your judo techniques. When you train, then, it is important that you plan and carry out exercises that will help your judo techniques develop and that will have direct application in your judo practice sessions.

TRAINING PRINCIPLES

When training, the following five principles should be strictly observed:

Overload
  • Lift weights that are over a certain level.

Gradualness
  • Increase weight and strength gradually.

Continuity
  • Train for an extended period of time.

Motivation
  • Understand why you train and conduct your trainings voluntarily and with enthusiasm.

Individuality and totality
  • Train in the way that suits you best and work for a total training program.

TRAINING METHODS

Adjust the weights you use according to your objectives:
  • To foster muscular strength, pull or lift up as fast as possible and use a weight that is one-third as heavy as your maximum muscular strength.
  • To foster power, use a weight that is about two-thirds as heavy as your maximum muscular strength and that you can lift from 8 to 10 times.

A

B

C

D

Diagonal pull-up

Training without Equipment

STRENGTHENING THE UPPER BODY

PUSH-UPS: Bend your elbows all the way down and straighten them up. Push-ups don't take much space and are representative, supplementary exercises which anyone can do.

A. Conduct push-ups with one hand.
B. Put a load on your back.
C. Keep your feet high.
D. Push up into the air and do a handclap.

DIAGONAL PULL-UPS: Clasp hands with your partner and pull up with your arms to raise your upper body.

A

B

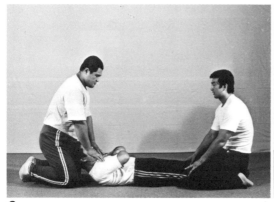

C

STRENGTHENING THE STOMACH (sit-ups)
Lie on your back and raise your upper body.

    A. Fix your knees and the lower parts of your legs so that they do not move.

    B. Place your feet on your partner's shoulders.

    C. Place weight on both of your shoulders.

Running carry

A

B

STRENGTHENING THE BACK AND LEGS

RUNNING CARRY: Hold your partner, lean back, and run an appropriate distance.

UPPER BODY BEND

A. From a standing position, clasp your partner and, with your back still straight, bend your upper body backward.

B. Lie with your face down and let your partner hold your lower legs. Then lift up your upper body.

Side hurdling

Squat

SIDE HURDLING: Leap over your partner, who is lying flat. Don't stop between jumps. For one set, do about 20 back-and-forth leaps.

SQUAT: Let your partner ride on your shoulders as you squat and stand up. Keep your back straight. This exercise creates a solid foundation for *seoi nage* and other throws using both feet.

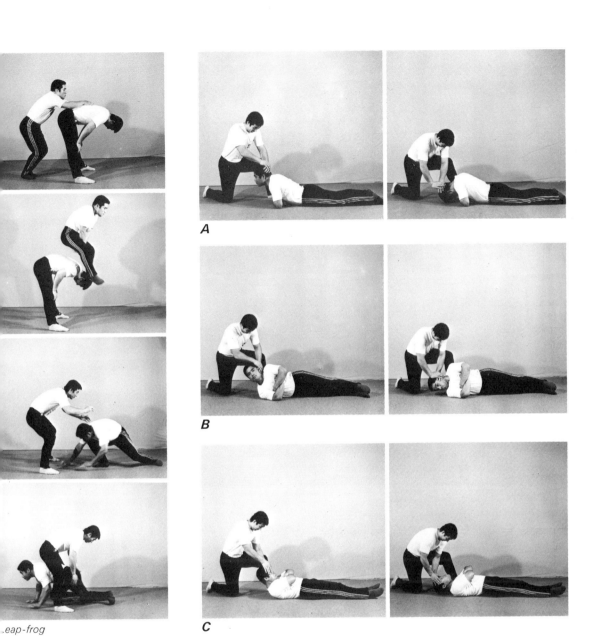

*eap-frog

A

B

C

STRENGTHENING THE BODY AND FOSTERING SPEED (leap-frog)

Leap over your partner from behind; then reverse your direction swiftly and crawl back through his legs. Perform this exercise without stopping for about 15 times to make one set.

STRENGTHENING THE NECK (neck press)

Let your partner push on your head with enough power to bend your neck down. Lower your neck while supporting the power pushing down and then raise your neck to press the pushing hand upward.

    A. The push comes from behind.
    B. The push comes from the side (alternate right and left).
    C. The push comes from the front.

Bench press   **1**   **2**

Back press   **1**   **2**

1

2

3

Dumbbell press

Training with Equipment

STRENGTHENING THE UPPER BODY

BENCH PRESS: The bench press is one of the most representative exercises for strengthening the muscles. The goal is to train so that you are capable of lifting at least your own body weight.

1. Lie on a bench. Grip the barbell with your hands about the width of your shoulders apart and place it on your chest.

2. Press it straight upward.

BACK PRESS: Sit down on a bench and, without using your legs, press up the barbell from behind your neck.

1. Place the barbell behind your neck.

2. Press it up straight over your head. Keep your back straight.

DUMBBELL PRESS: Raise the dumbbell alternately. This exercise is good for strengthening your *tsurite*.

1. Hold the dumbbells with both hands next to your shoulders.

2. Straighten one arm and press the dumbbell over your head.

3. Let the dumbbell down as you press up the other dumbbell. Repeat this exercise, alternating arms.

A

B

C

CHEST AND WAIST PULLS: Conducted with great speed, chest and waist pulls will strengthen the "pull" and "push" which are so important in judo. This is a power training method that has great application in actual judo combat.

A. Pull with one hand. Use your entire body.

B. Pull with both hands. Alternate good *hikite* and *tsurite* combinations.

C. Train your *tsurite*.

Barbell curl   *1*   *2*

Dumbbell curl   *1*   *2*   *3*   *4*

Upright rowing   *1*   *2*

BARBELL CURL: Train by curling a barbell up to shoulder level.

1. Stand up while gripping the barbell with your palms facing front.

2. Keep your elbows close to your side and curl the barbell up to shoulder level.

DUMBBELL CURL: Alternating hands, curl the dumbbells up to shoulder level.

1. Hold the dumbbells in both hands.

2. Curl up one dumbbell to the level of your shoulder.

3, 4. As you lower one dumbbell, raise the other.

UPRIGHT ROWING: Hoist a barbell to the level of your shoulders. This strengthens the power of the *hikite*.

1. Stand up while holding the barbell squarely with your hands together.

2. Hoist the barbell swiftly in one stroke up to the level of your shoulder. At this point, your bent elbows are at ear level.

Bent-over rowing

Arm pull-over

BENT-OVER ROWING: Bend your upper body forward with your back straight and lift the barbell to your stomach and chest. This exercise will strengthen your pulling power and will also help develop the muscles all over your body.

1. Bend your upper body forward and grasp the barbell.

2, 3. With your back straight, pull up the barbell to your stomach and chest.

ARM PULL-OVER: Lie on your back on a bench. Lower the barbell over your shoulders to the back of your head and then raise it up again. There are two ways of doing this exercise—while bending the arms and while keeping them straight.

1. Lie on your back on a bench and hold the barbell over your chest with both hands.

2, 3. Lift the barbell around your shoulders and lower it behind your head in a half-circle motion. Then raise and return the barbell to its former position.

Training with Equipment **219**

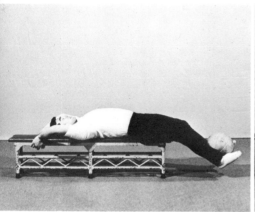

Bench leg raise   *1*   *2*   *3*

Dead lift   *1*   *2*   *3*

STRENGTHENING THE STOMACH (bench leg raise)

Hold a medicine ball between your feet and lift it up. Do the exercise without a medicine ball until you have gotten used to the movement. This exercise is good for strengthening your stomach muscles and also provides effective training for *nage-waza* and *katamewaza*.

1. Lie on a bench with your legs hanging off the end. Hold a medicine ball with both of your feet and grip the edges of the bench firmly with both hands.

2, 3. With your legs extended straight out, raise them up (together with the medicine ball) until they are vertical.

STRENGTHENING THE BACK AND LEGS

DEAD LIFT: Raise your upper body while holding the barbell.

1. Spread your feet and bend your knees to grasp the barbell.

2. While raising your upper body, straighten your knees.

3. Lean backward.

Ball toss   **1**   **2**   **3**

A Full squat

B Half squat

BALL TOSS: You need two partners. The one who throws the ball throws it to the catcher's left, right, and middle. Use a light ball at first and gradually move on to heavier ones. Vary the speed of the throw.

1. Lie face down on a bench with your upper body extending over the edge. Have one partner hold your legs firmly.

2. The partner facing you throws the ball.

3. Catch the ball and throw it back to your partner. (Don't let the ball touch the floor.)

SQUAT: With the barbell on your shoulders, squat and rise up. A judoist must have strong legs and hip muscles as well as good *bane* (spring). Squats are one of the best methods for developing these qualities. They also provide good training for *seoi nage* and *tsurikomi goshi*.

A. Full squat: Spread your legs a shoulder-width apart and lay the barbell on your shoulders. With your back straight, bend your knees and squat way down. Then stand up.

B. Half squat: This is done like the full squat except the knees are only bent until they form a 90° angle.

Bench hurdle   **1**   **2**   **3**

Flying split

Jumping squat

BENCH HURDLE: With your knees bent, jump over the bench from left to right and vice versa. Gradually make the bench higher and increase the speed of the jumps.

1. Crouch down by the side of the bench.

2, 3. With both of your feet close together, use the spring of your knees to jump over the bench sideways.

FLYING SPLIT: Shoulder the barbell and jump up; then split the legs (one forward and the other backward) as you come down and lower your hips. Alternate your legs back and front. Using a light weight and doing the exercise speedily will be most effective for increasing the power of your *uchimata* and other leg techniques as well as the power in your legs and hips.

JUMPING SQUAT: Stand up with the barbell on your shoulders and take a big jump forward. Spread out your legs to the left and right and lower your hips as you contact the floor.

igh clean   **1**   **2**   **3**   **4**

High clean and press

STRENGTHENING THE WHOLE BODY

HIGH CLEAN: Raise the barbell up to the height of your chest. This is an exercise for your whole body and strengthens the muscles of your arms, shoulders, chest, back, and legs.

1. Straighten your back and bend your hips and knees. Grip the barbell with your hands a shoulder-width apart.

2, 3. Straighten out your hips and knees to raise the barbell.

4. Swing both elbows forward and upward and catch the barbell on your chest. Keep your back straight.

HIGH CLEAN AND PRESS: Do a "high clean" and then raise the barbell over your head.

1
4
2
3
5

BALL TOSS: Toss a medicine ball with your partner back and forth. Stand at some distance from your partner and use your entire body to throw the ball from every conceivable angle—from below, from above, to the side, on a diagonal, and so on. This exercise not only strengthens the whole body but also provides a period of relaxation before and after judo training.

224 Training

6

Judo and I

All the techniques presented in this book, though perfectly suited for recreation in themselves, are in essence designed for hand-to-hand battle against an opponent. The object in such a contest is to win. And in order to win in the arena you have to think of the match as a fight against yourself as much as a fight against the opponent. Throwing every bit of yourself into the battle for the sake of victory is where the real attraction and excitement of judo come from. In this chapter the authors would like to reveal some of their thoughts about judo, their life in the sport, and the qualities they believe a winning style demands.

Isao Inokuma (left) advising
Yasuhiro Yamashita.

At the Tokai University judo club.

Fighting Spirit   *Isao Inokuma*

I started learning judo at the age of fifteen, intent on becoming another Sanshiro
Sugata, the great master of judo who has been depicted in Japanese novels and
movies and on television. Since then, I have spent my life involved in judo and have
learned many lessons from the sport.

I believe I can roughly divide my career as a judoist into three periods. The first
period sees me entering Riichiro Watanabe-sensei's *dojo* in the city of Yokosuka,
still a boy and intent on becoming a strong judoist. The second period includes my
first participation in the All-Japan Judo Tournament. I broke the jinx that said a
newcomer would never win the tournament, and in so doing also established a
record as the youngest man ever to win the title of judo champion of Japan. This second period also includes my winning the heavyweight-class judo championship in
the 1964 Tokyo Olympic Games and the open-division title in the Fourth World
Judo Tournament in 1965. The third period covers the days up to the present and
my work as an instructor developing promising young judoists. In each of these
three periods I have concentrated all of my efforts and enthusiasm on judo.

But when I was a child I was rather sickly and did not have much of a physique.
Also, I was not very agile or dexterous. The only weapon I had at my disposal, then,
was a fighting spirit—a spirit which gave me the confidence that I would not be
defeated by anyone. And I think it fair to say that it is this fighting spirit which
characterized my judo throughout my career. I had good *ippon seoi nage* and *tai
otoshi,* but it was because of my fighting spirit that these techniques proved effective against my opponents.

As a boy, as an active judoist, and as an instructor, I have experienced a great
many things, all of which I can hardly relate here. Based on my experiences, however, I will jot down some of my observations about judo.

Kaminaga vs. Inokuma. The final match of the All-Japan Judo Tournament, 1959.

Never Give Up

Judo is a combative sport. It is a martial art aimed at defeating your opponent. Other purposes of judo involve developing physical strength and mental spirit. But when you are up against an opponent, you must never forget the combative aspect of the sport. You fight against your opponent, throwing him down to the mat to achieve victory. At the same time, you fight against yourself. If you think your opponent is stronger than you and get the jitters, or if you are in a difficult position and feel that you must give up, then it will be impossible for you to win. You must not give up the bout until the last second, no matter how strong your opponent may be. You must have a fighting spirit which will urge you on to attack and attack again to the very end. Fighting spirit, to put it simply, is the first thing a judoist needs.

Of course, I cannot deny that you may feel anxiety or uneasiness before a fight. Feelings like "I don't want to be beaten," "I just want to run away," or "I'm frightened" are always felt to a certain degree. Also there is loneliness. But what is important during these times is not to be afraid of loneliness, anxiety, or weakness of the will but to overwhelm these feelings with a fierce fighting spirit and confront your opponent with your intention to defeat him.

I experienced such anxiety and overcame it when I participated in my first All-Japan Judo Tournament.

It was 1959. I was a senior at Tokyo University of Education and was unknown as a judoist. Furthermore, I was the smallest man in the tournament, weighing only 83 kilograms and standing 173 centimeters tall. As I mentioned, there was a belief that no newcomer could ever win the tournament. My opponent in my first preliminary bout was Yuzo Oda, a giant of a man—193 centimeters tall and weighing 100 kilograms. Because Oda had been touted as a sure winner of the tournament, no one believed I had any chance of beating him.

Before I fought Oda I was deep in thought for a long time. After considering it over and over, I decided that the best strategy would be to launch an attack against Oda time and time again, relentlessly. My idea was to "do or die," and I hoped to discover a way to win by hammering away on the offensive, as is suggested in the old Japanese saying, "Attacking is the best defense."

Yasuhiro Yamashita on his way to defeating Turin at the Jigoro Kano Cup Tournament, 1978.

In order to carry out this strategy it was necessary for me to have the stamina to continue my attacks, as well as the fighting spirit that would enable me to generate such stamina. By nature, I disliked being beaten by the other fellow, and since I had built up my stamina during practice sessions, I attacked Oda without fear. As a result, my strategy proved successful, and after fighting for the full time I won the bout with *yusei gachi* (judge's decision). This was a very important victory for me and signified the first step toward the maturation of my judo. Also, from this victory, my confidence increased considerably in regard to my notion that one must always go on the offensive in judo.

After winning my first bout with Oda, I won all my other matches up to the finals. And by defeating my opponent in the finals my confidence in my judo increased even more. My opponent here was Akio Kaminaga, another man thought to have a good chance of winning the tournament. He, too, had won all of his matches up to the finals.

By the time of my bout with Kaminaga, all of my stamina was depleted and I was resting in a very exhausted state in the dressing room, muttering words to the effect that I couldn't possibly win. Hearing these words, Watanabe-sensei scolded me sharply. Encouraged by his scolding, I went up to the judo arena. My match with Kaminaga proceeded with him in a superior position, but about one minute before the end the big clock in the arena caught my eye as I returned to the mat.

I thought to myself, I must beat him with my favorite *ippon seoi nage* before the time is up. As soon as I grabbed hold of Kaminaga, I pushed him backward to get him into position. Up to then, Kaminaga had thwarted all such attempts of mine. But this time, when I pushed him backward, he moved forward together with my push; taking advantage of this, I made the throw. The hall was in an uproar, and after several moments the chief referee declared my *seoi nage* a *waza ari* (half point). Thus I had managed to come from behind to win the title of the All-Japan Judo Tournament.

My victory was the result of my never giving up the match until the very end. There are some judoists who are quite strong during practice sessions but who fail to live up to their expectations in competition. There are also judoists who in a

The author throwing Yoshizawa with ippon seoi nage at the All-Japan Judo Tournament, 1960.

match are unable to execute the techniques that they are actually in full possession of. The problems here lie in the attitudes of these men before the fights begin : They defeat themselves before they enter the judo arena. Only by using all your energy and spirit until the very last can you win a bout. I become more certain of this each time I watch Yasuhiro Yamashita.

Yamashita is one of my protégés. He is also the one who broke my record as the youngest judoist to win the All-Japan Judo Tournament. Yamashita is not only a big man, but also a fighter who likes to train very hard. During the Jigoro Kano Cup International Judo Tournament held at the Nippon Budokan (Tokyo) in November 1978, Yamashita exhibited fully a fighting spirit that simply overwhelmed his opponents on his way to winning the open-class title. The open-class bouts were held on the fourth and last day of the tournament. Aside from Yamashita, those participating were Novikov of the Soviet Union, winner of the open-class title in the Montreal Olympics, Rouge (France), Adler (the Netherlands), and other top-flight judoists of the world.

In his second bout, Yamashita met the big Russian Turin. Yamashita had a hard time getting his techniques to work because Turin continued to take strong defensive positions. Yamashita was taken for a *koka* (two steps below a *waza ari*) when Turin countered with a technique after Yamashita had attacked. The spectators in the hall gasped when the *koka* was proclaimed, and everyone thought that the seemingly invincible Yamashita would go down to defeat. But Yamashita redoubled his attacks against Turin, who maintained his defense with his long arms. Several seconds before the match was over, Yamashita unleashed *o-uchi gari* to pick up a *yuko* (between *koka* and *waza ari*) and a victory.

During the finals, Yamashita met Rouge of France, and although the techniques of the two men were ineffective, it was clear that Yamashita was the more aggressive and that the bout was in his favor. Yet Yamashita continued his relentless attack against Rouge and just before the end of the match he caught him with *o-soto gari* to gain a *yuko* and the title as well. It was a brilliant strategy on the part of Yamashita.

The spirit of a combative sport is that one does not give up until the very end and keeps up a relentless attack against the opponent. Always take a bold, forward

Defeating Muto with tai otoshi at the All-Japan Judo Tournament, 1960.

posture and sweep away your fears. No matter what the situation may be, as long as you have a fighting spirit and the desire to win you will always discover a way to victory.

Build up Your Body and Your Techniques

You may have fighting spirit, but if you don't combine it with excellent techniques you can't win a bout. It is often said that *shin-gi-tai* (spirit, skill, and power) is necessary to win in judo. You have to train hard so that these three elements will be in harmony with each other when you face your opponent in the judo arena. Hard training will not only dispose of your anxieties, but it will also create physical strength and fighting spirit, thus enabling you to fight with everything you have.

I have often noted when viewing international judo tournaments in recent years that Japanese judoists are inferior to their foreign counterparts in basic physical powers and, as a result, lose their bouts without being able to apply their techniques to the fullest. There is a saying which gets to the heart of judo: *Ju yoku go o seisu* (Softness overcomes hardness). There are some who, hearing this, believe that even without strength they can defeat their opponents. But this is false. How can a man who has not trained diligently or who has not built up his physical strength defeat his opponent? Adages like "Softness overcomes hardness" or "A small man can defeat a big man" only apply when your basic physical powers are on a par with the opponent's; in such a situation, power is not the issue, and it is here that we first glimpse the importance of the smooth working of *shin-gi-tai* in a match.

It is my opinion that the techniques of Japanese judoists today are more varied and on a higher level than those of their foreign counterparts. But in order for these techniques to be truly effective, Japanese judoists have to develop basic physical powers that are in no way inferior to anyone else's.

Many foreign judoists on the scene today possess not only excellent basic physical powers but also strong techniques that have overwhelmed their Japanese opponents time and time again. Among the foreign judoists with brilliant *shin-gi-tai* are the Soviet Union's Nevzorov, the victor in the light-middleweight class in the Montreal Olympics, Dvoinikov of the Soviet Union, who was runnerup in the

Winning with ippon seoi nage against Hasegawa at the All-Japan Judo Tournament, 1963.

middleweight division at the same Olympics, and Lorentz of East Germany, who won the 95-kilograms-and-under class in the Jigoro Kano Cup International Judo Tournament held in Tokyo in 1978.

Because I was small physically, I took up weight training during my boyhood in order to overcome this handicap and strengthen my body. With my new power, and in combination with my favorite techniques—*seoi nage* and *tai otoshi*—I built up my own judo. I believe that a small man like me was able to beat bigger men because I was able to back up my favorite techniques with basic physical power.

A judoist's strongest and best techniques become his weapons during a contest. Being strong, the more authority in their execution the more effective the result. But it takes a long time and some very hard practice to develop techniques that you can truly call your own. My favorite techniques were *seoi nage* and *tai otoshi*. Both involve heaving up the opponent from below. I learned them from Watanabe-sensei, who often used to tell me that if a small man is to defeat a big man, the small man must practice and master *katsugiwaza,* or carrying techniques.

I was never one for exhibiting brilliant judo techniques. But as far as my *ippon seoi nage* was concerned, I was always sure I could bring down my opponent, no matter who he was or what the situation, as long as I caught him in exactly the position I wanted him.

Power, speed, and stamina are going to be particularly important in judo from now on. Becoming able to win a judo match will involve adding basic physical training to your daily practice to develop these qualities as well as working to master techniques of devastating effectiveness.

Don't Stop Learning

Let us say that you have mastered a certain technique and are meeting an opponent. If you depend only on your favorite technique, the time will surely come when it will not work and you will find it difficult to win. This is because your opponent has thoroughly studied your technique as well as the flow of your matches and has devised countermeasures to neutralize you.

During the All-Japan Judo Tournament held in 1959, I concentrated on *seoi nage*

Attacking Sakaguchi with ippon seoi nage at the All-Japan Judo Tournament, 1963.

to win, but in the championship of the following year I tasted a bitter defeat. The reason for this is that my opponents had studied my *seoi nage* thoroughly and were on their guard from the very start. I managed to win up to the finals by virtue of my determination, but in my bout with Akio Kaminaga, the man I had defeated the previous year, all my *seoi nage* were thwarted and I ended up in defeat. This showed me that you can't win by always fighting with the same pattern of attack, technique, and strategy. In order to win and continue winning, you must study and work much harder than your opponent.

I realized then and there that I must perfect a technique other than *seoi nage*. This was to be *tai otoshi*. Unlike in *seoi nage,* in *tai otoshi* you do not throw your opponent directly in front of you but twist your body a little to the side. You have to unbalance the opponent with good timing first. In *seoi nage,* there is the fear that your opponent may thwart you by hugging you and then countering with his own technique. But in *tai otoshi* this fear is slight. I thought that if I perfected *tai otoshi* and mixed it with *seoi nage* I could execute either one of them as the occasion demanded and keep the opponent from knowing which one I planned to use. As a result, the opponent would not know how to best guard himself against me. Naturally I worked at *o-uchi gari* and *ko-uchi gari* strenuously until they also became techniques I could use. By using these leg techniques to get the opponent off-balance, I established several attack patterns that could lead into *seoi nage* or *tai otoshi*.

I also practiced my mat techniques very hard. My goal was to execute them quickly in combination with my standing techniques to ensure victory. By studying and strengthening my work on the mat, I managed to eliminate the anxiety I had felt about it and could thus carry out my standing techniques boldly and without any apprehension.

In 1961 I hurt my hip and had to spend some time recovering from the injury. When I got well, I practiced mat techniques diligently. As a result, I succeeded in winning the All-Judo Tournament for the second time in 1963.

My strategy in the tournament was to concentrate on mat techniques after executing a standing technique. Also, when the opponent attempted a technique, I

Sending Kaseya to the mat with ippon seoi nage at the 1964 Tokyo Olympics.

would counter him and drag him down on the mat so that I could grapple with him there. Because I was confident in my mat techniques and because I was sure that I could fight on a par with my opponent even if I was the one thrown down to the mat, I was able to attack with my favorite *seoi nage* purposefully and without fear.

I always studied my opponents far in advance, and when an opponent was bigger than me I would hold him so that his eyes would be at the same level as mine. The results of my study bore fruit in the first International Judo Tournament held in Moscow in March 1961 when I fought Kiknadze of the Soviet Union.

This tournament was kind of a preliminary to the soon-to-come Tokyo Olympics of 1964, when judo was to be included in the competition for the first time. The tournament was also a good opportunity for me to see whether my *tai otoshi* would be effective against foreign judoists. The favorites in the tournament were Kiknadze and myself. Kiknadze was an enormous man, capable of firing an automatic rifle with only one hand or lifting me clear up off the ground. I met him twice, once in the preliminary league and once in the finals. In the preliminaries I defeated Kiknadze in a matter of 30 seconds with *ippon seoi nage*. I couldn't have been more astounded at the victory. However, Kiknadze managed to win all of his other bouts and I had to confront him again in the finals. It seemed that he had been studying my *ippon seoi nage*, for when I pushed him backward, he would not push back at me. He would instead block the movement of my right hand with his left hand. I got pretty flustered and, breaking my customary rhythm, I attempted *ippon seoi nage* just as Kiknadze was stepping back. He seemed to have been waiting for just this opportunity, because he hugged me tightly and executed a strong back throw. It was judged a *waza ari*.

You can imagine my disappointment. I was bound to lose if I did not make use of everything I had been studying up till then. I decided to attack with a mixture of *seoi nage* and *tai otoshi*. This proved effective. After five minutes, I attempted a *seoi nage* in the same pattern as before, and, like the previous time, Kiknadze tried to hug me. I took this opportunity to lower my body and switched to *tai otoshi*. Kiknadze fell to the mat from his right hip down. It was a *waza ari*. We were now equal. Kiknadze put caution to the wind and came forward voluntarily. He was in a

Receiving the gold medal at the award ceremonies of the 1964 Tokyo Olympics.

position to be caught with my *seoi nage,* but this time I faked *seoi nage* and changed to *tai otoshi.* It was a perfect *ippon.* If I had not studied *tai otoshi* I would probably have lost to Kiknadze in this bout.

In judo you will meet many kinds of opponents. The types of techniques they use are also very different, depending on their physiques. In order to continue winning against such a wide variety of opponents you must study and train harder than they do. A person who engages in the same type of training every day, who fights the same types of contest every day, and who loses in the same way every day will never be able to develop a winning pattern. I hope everyone who reads this essay will keep this in mind.

Use Your Judo in Your Daily Life

In the Tokyo Olympics held in October 1964, I won the heavyweight title. The following year I won the open-class title at the Fourth World Judo Tournament held in Brazil to end my career as an active judoist. I am now retired from competition. While I am concentrating on developing promising young judoists, I am also trying to lead a life that shows how the spirit of judo can be brought into one's daily behavior. I am trying to apply to society the same judo spirit that I acquired during my years of training. My attitude at my place of work is the same as that when I was practicing at a *dojo* or was engaged in contests in the arena. I am putting all my enthusiasm and fighting spirit into my current work and keeping up my studies. Judo is not a sport to be engaged in only at the *dojo.*

Jigoro Kano-sensei trained on the principle that one can attain his objective by getting both his spirit and body to work together productively. And he said that one of the major objectives of judo training was to become able to apply this principle to all aspects of life in society. With "fighting spirit" as my motto, I am even now, in the *dojo* that is society, drawing from my past judo experience to pursue my studies further. "Fighting spirit" judo is, for me, a life-long endeavor.

Nobuyuki Sato applying sankaku tojime to Kaneko at the All-Japan Judo Tournament, 1975.

Never Say Die!

Nobuyuki Sato

One encounters many things in life, and from these encounters one learns a great deal as one grows into adulthood. As I reminisce about my past, I cannot help but be struck by the wonderful people I have met, the good teachers I have had, and the good friends I have made. I think I have led a very happy life and am thankful for it.

What I am today is all due to my brother Nobuhiro, who is four years older than me. He and I walked virtually the same path from kindergarten to college, and after finishing school, we continued along the same course, teaching judo at Tokai University. For me, Nobuhiro was my goal. He was everything. When he was in senior high school he started practicing judo in earnest. I saw how diligently he worked and made up mind then and there to follow in his footsteps and become as strong as he was. This was my motive for starting to learn judo.

My father and mother also were deeply interested in and understood the importance of physical education. My father was a professor of physical education (track and field) at Hokkaido University of Arts and Sciences, while my mother had been a swimming star during her high school days.

My start in judo was a good one. While my brother had not had a teacher, I began judo at an earlier age than he did and had him to serve as my guide. And he guided me well. When I was in the third year of junior high school, Nobuhiro was attending Tokyo University of Education and was a member of its judo club. During school vacations, he used to return to Hokkaido and teach me judo. He also passed on a lot of information about the judo circles in Tokyo. You can imagine how eager I was to learn what was going on there, the center of the judo world, and how stimulated I was by what I heard. When the vacation ended and my brother had to return to school in Tokyo, he always gave me some work to be completed by the time he

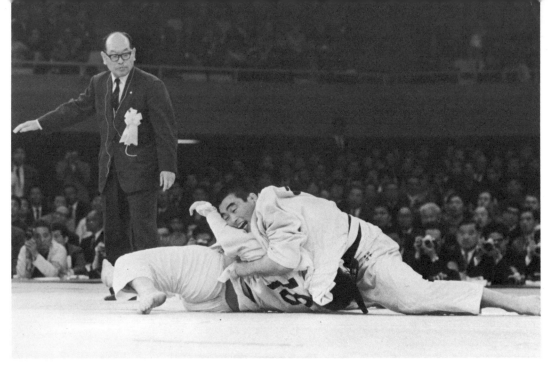

Holding K. Sato in kuzure kami shiho gatame at the All-Japan Judo Tournament, 1968

returned to Hokkaido on his next vacation. If there was anything about judo I didn't understand, I would write to him and he would send me his answer.

When I entered the Hakodate Chubu Senior High School in Hokkaido, my biggest goal was to become high school champion of the whole of Hokkaido. During my junior high school days, I had not participated in any judo tournament outside the school because we did not have any judo instructor. I did not know how much ability I had since my only opponents had been my classmates. My brother, who saw in me the talents and abilities of a future judoist, drew up a list of things for me to accomplish while I was in high school. I was to become a first *dan* (grade) by the summer of my freshman year, to become second *dan* by the summer of my junior year, and to become the judo champion of all of Hokkaido's high schools in my senior year. This was a schedule my brother himself had dreamed of following but had not been able to. My brother was always boasting to others that I would someday become a judo champion, and I lived up to his expectations when I finally did become the judo champion of all the high schools in Hokkaido in my senior year.

I was never first in sports or scholarships during my elementary and junior high school days. There was always someone who was better than me no matter what I did. And since I had a very strong will to win, my position as less than best was hard to tolerate. When I became the high school judo champion of Hokkaido, however, I realized that if I had the will I could succeed in anything I wanted to. I was brimming with confidence: number one in my high school, then in the city of Hakodate, then in all of Hokkaido. I devoted myself to training more and more.

In this same senior year in high school, the first individual judo tournament was held in commemoration of the Tenth Inter–High School Judo Tournament. Although my school was defeated in the school competition, I captured the individual championship and, as a result, qualified to participate in the All-Japan Student Judo Tournament. I was confident that I would make a good showing, but during the preliminary league tournament I lost in the drawing of lots. After that I participated in the National Athletic Tournament, but this time also I lost in the drawings in my second bout. I had lost twice, but I was still confident that I could

Taking down Ueno with o-soto gari at the All-Japan Judo Tournament, 1968.

make a good showing in Tokyo, and my yearning to go there to improve my techniques became stronger each day.

My high school was known for turning out many students who were able to pass the grueling entrance exams to universities, and the pressure of study left the school's judo club in great need of members. The manager of the club was Seiichiro Misawa-sensei. His motto was *Shinken naru doryoku* (Do your utmost). He used to tell us judo club members that, as long as we practiced judo seriously, short periods of practice would be sufficient and we would be able to mix sports with our studies. He also noted that physical power was one prerequisite for passing entrance exams. Together with Misawa-sensei, we used to roam the school to solicit new members for our judo club. This is one of the fondest memories I have of my high school days.

Like my brother, who graduated that year, I entered Tokyo University of Education and became a member of the judo club. My first goal was to become a regular member of the club, that is, to qualify to participate in judo tournaments as a regular member of the school team. Another target was to be able to participate in the All-Japan Judo Tournament while I was still a student.

The manager of the judo club at that time was Isao Inokuma-sensei. When I was in my sophomore year in college, he won the All-Japan Judo Tournament for the second time, and in the following year he took the heavyweight championship in the Tokyo Olympics. He was at the peak of his career. Having the opportunity to train with Inokuma-sensei, I put my whole body and soul into judo. Practice was severe beyond words. I was thrown down on the mat so violently so many times that I thought for sure I would never survive. Nevertheless, I charged into Inokuma-sensei with a ferocious vigor. By practicing with him and by watching the contests in which he participated, I came to know his brand of judo, which overflowed with vitality. But at the same time I felt privileged to have Inokuma-sensei as my instructor, I also felt that I must become as strong as he was.

I sprained my knee before entering college, and for three months after I became a freshman I could not practice judo. In my junior year I was laid up for several months because of a herniated disc. Except for these two mishaps, I was lucky to

On the mat with Endo in the semifinals of the All-Japan Judo Tournament, 1974.

be able to practice regularly. In high school, since the school was located in Hokkaido and we had to study hard for the college entrance exams, I had not had much time for practice, but in college my life centered wholly on judo. There were practices at the school, at the Kodokan, at the Tokyo Metropolitan Police Department. "I want to become strong in judo" were the words that formed my every thought.

I was told by Inokuma-sensei to foster a scientific eye toward judo. During our school's practice session in Tottori, when I was a freshman, I had the opportunity to meet Mitsuo Kimura-sensei, who was famous for his *sankaku jime* and who had been active during his college days as a brilliant judoist. Whenever Kimura-sensei came to Tokyo, I would knock at his door and ask him to teach me his famous mat techniques. I even went to Tottori to take lessons from him.

I started off in judo with my brother as my goal, and I finally began to beat him around the summer of my junior year in college when I grappled with him during summer vacation. Also in my junior year, my father died and our family was faced with a financial crisis. But my mother and brother provided me with enough funds to enable me to continue my judo training without having to take a side job. I would be in a different position today were it not for the help they gave me.

When I was a senior, I qualified to participate in the All-Japan Judo Tournament and this gave me immense satisfaction, for it fulfilled one of my greatest hopes. Upon graduation from college, I planned to teach at a senior high school in my native Hakodate. But after an excellent showing at the All-Japan Judo Tournament, I made up my mind to win the tournament sometime in the future and decided to stay in Tokyo where there were many tough training partners.

Under these circumstances, I was employed by Hakuhodo, a public relations company that had a strong judo team and that was then emerging as a potential contender for the judo championship among the Japanese business firms. The manager of Hakuhodo's judo club was Kazunari Onda-sensei, an earlier graduate of my own alma mater. Onda-sensei was a mathematician whose way of thinking was theoretical and unique. He studied and analyzed in great detail each judo technique and all kinds of combination plays, combat strategies, and control methods, and

Bringing down Ninomiya for the championship of the All-Japan Judo Tournament, 1974.

then conveyed to us what he had observed. He also taught us how to conduct ourselves as members of society and created an atmosphere where we could practice judo to our hearts' content even while we were employed by a company.

At Hakuhodo I put all my energy into judo, and it was in August 1966 that I was finally recognized as a first-class judoist by virtue of my participation in the heavy-weight championship bout in the First Weight-Classified Judo Tournament. In my first match, I defeated the veteran Koga with *kuzure kami shiho gatame.* In the semifinals I beat the giant Sakaguchi with the same technique. But in the finals I was beaten by a slight margin by Matsunaga, the All-Japan champion of 1966. I was the runner-up in the tournament, but I found out that I could do equal battle with top-ranking judoists and that my techniques were not inferior to theirs. As a result of this tournament, not only I but others as well began to think I had a chance of capturing the All-Japan championship.

In the fall of 1966, I was selected as a judo representative of Tokyo for the National Athletic Tournament held in Oita. I won every bout I had with first-class opponents and became more and more confident of winning the All-Japan crown.

During the All-Japan Judo Tournament held the following year (1967) I won every one of my bouts and met Isao Okano in the finals. Okano defeated me by getting a *waza ari* for his *ippon seoi nage.* It was a great disappointment to lose to an opponent who was smaller than me.

That summer I participated in the Fifth World Judo Tournament held at Salt Lake City and won first honors in the class of 93 kilograms and under. In the 1968 All-Japan Judo Tournament, everyone thought that Okano and I would fight for the championship, but, regrettably, Matsuzaka defeated me in the semifinals by *ko-mata sukui.* In the All-Japan Weight Classified Tournament, however, I entered the heavyweight class and managed to win the title.

In January, 1969, I left Hakuhodo and was employed by Tokai University as a judo instructor. I had always wanted to become a teacher, and though I had attended a government-supported school, I was impressed by the vitality of private universities. Tokai had established a new martial arts department that focused on judo, and I was attracted by the opportunity to try to help build up the judo club

Receiving congratulations from Shigeyoshi Matsumae, President of Tokai University.

from practically nothing into one of the foremost in Japan. I did not hesitate for a moment, then, when Inokuma-sensei, my senior and teacher, invited me to take the post as instructor of judo at the university. Of course, I had every intention of continuing my career as an active judoist.

After joining the staff of Tokai University, I set up two targets—to win the All-Japan Judo Tournament and to make Tokai University's judo team the champion of all university teams in Japan. With strong support from Tokai President Matsumae, Inokuma-sensei, and other teachers and colleagues, I pursued these objectives with all the energy I had.

I was defeated in the preliminaries of the 1969 All-Japan Judo Tournament, and in 1970 all I could do was finish among the best eight. In 1971 I was the runner-up and in 1972, third. I placed among the best sixteen in the 1973 tournament. But I just couldn't seem to win it.

In the meantime my other achievements were : third place in the 1969 World Judo Tournament (all-weight class), winner of the 93-kilogram class in the 1971 All-Japan Weight-Classified Judo Tournament, second place in the 1971 World Judo Tournament (93-kilogram class), and champion of the 93-kilogram class in the 1973 World Judo Tournament. But no All-Japan championship ! It was still just a dream, and I thought about it day and night. Frankly, I was in a rather unbalanced state of mind. One voice told me I simply did not have the ability to win, while another told me to continue my efforts and wait until the following year.

For the 1974 All-Japan Judo Tournament, my condition was the worst it had been since 1967. In January of 1974 I caught a cold which nearly developed into pneumonia, wrecking my condition. My training, both in amount and quality, had been very poor, and my physical powers had greatly deteriorated. I made up my mind that, win or lose, 1974 would see my last participation in the All-Japan Judo Tournament. Others were also thinking the same thing. Therefore, I told myself that I would do battle in each bout as if it were the very last one I would engage in. It was the first time that I told myself it would be my last tournament. I don't know whether this determination had anything to do with the results, but at last I managed to win.

Winning the championship of the European Sambo Tournament, 1972

Afterward, I told myself that ability alone cannot win a tournament. Destiny also plays a big role in judo.

My advice, from my own experience, is not to give up. "If you set up a target, strive to accomplish it no matter what happens. Destiny will surely be on your side some day." These are the words made famous by Jigoro Kano-sensei.

Untiring Efforts Make the Man

During the time I was actively participating in judo competitions, no one ever told me I had the talents or abilities of a judoist or that I had any sense of judo. Judo, I think, is a matter of all-around power, and this holds true for any other sport. Though your feeling for judo may not be the best, you can overtake an opponent with good judo sense by practicing twice or three times as hard as he does. The important thing is to be in possession of a fighting spirit, a never-say-die spirit. I believe that a person in possession of such a spirit and who also has good techniques and physical power will in the end emerge the victor. Making untiring efforts toward the accomplishment of a goal and developing a fighting spirit, I believe, also demand a kind of talent.

While I was still competing, I made up my mind to study various other sports and to do things others didn't in an attempt to adopt new ideas into my judo. One of the sports I studied was wrestling. From December 1966 to January 1967 I worked with a group of wrestlers training for the Olympics. During the practice sessions I studied holds and the development of basic physical power and was able to make use of what I learned in my own judo. Also from 1966, I began studying Russian sambo in earnest. In comparing sambo with judo, I found out that, on the whole, judo techniques were on a higher level. But I also discovered that the *ura nage* and *juji gatame* used in sambo were considerably more powerful and effective than those in judo. Another thing I noted was that because the stance in sambo is wide, the samboist is vulnerable to forward-and-back combination techniques, particularly to those like *tai otoshi, ko-uchi gari,* and *o-uchi gari.* Thus I was able to take advantage of the weak points of Russian judoists when I met them in contests. As the saying goes, to know your enemy and to know yourself is the way to victory.

On the way to the light-heavyweight title of the 8th World Judo Tournament, 1973.

I took up weight training on the advice of Inokuma-sensei during my student days. This proved of great value later and made it possible for me to build up a body with strong muscles. Furthermore, on the advice of my father, who told me that running was the basis of all sports, I ran whenever I had the time. I continued weight training and running to the last day I was in active competition.

I am often called "*newaza* Sato," and this is probably due to the characteristics of my body—very supple but without much spring in it. An opponent I held down on the mat would often say that it was like being pressed on by a glutinous hunk of Japanese rice cake. Another reason, perhaps, which made me good in mat techniques was that, during practice in cold Hokkaido, we often started out practicing mat techniques first so that we wouldn't get hurt later.

But you can't win just with mat techniques. It is my belief that you must be able to win with standing techniques as well. After all, if you feel confident about your work on the mat, you can execute a standing technique without fear of being countered, and your opponent, too, will hesitate to throw you down. Good mat techniques will bring you many advantages in your bouts and will enable you to battle your opponents without giving them any openings. But I advise you to master standing techniques, too, difficult as this may be.

When I was a student, I favored left holds and used to grab my opponent by his inner collar. However, this was not effective when I fought a very big man, so I lowered my left hand and heaved my opponent up from below. A beginner in judo is often influenced greatly by his teacher, but when he runs into a problem and doesn't know what to do, he has to find the solution himself and change his form by his own willpower and efforts.

Fight Like There's No Tomorrow

Since 1969 I have been teaching judo with Inokuma-sensei at Tokai University. I am very grateful to have the chance to teach the students of the judo club there and to foster promising youths. Our school won the team honors in the All-Japan Student Judo Tournament twice, and I have helped develop numerous students into judo champions. I have also had the opportunity to meet Yasuhiro Yamashita, one

As an instructor, watching his team.   *With Yasuhiro Yamashita at practice*

of the most promising judoists in Japan today. All my hopes have been realized since I started at the university, thanks to the organizational cooperation extended to me by President Matsumae and other teachers. I would like to express my deep gratitude to them.

As a teacher of judo, I hope that my students will always win. I hope they will always be confident of winning and will study the ways that they can win. In contests I want them to display all their power against their opponents. For this reason I urge my students to fight each battle with all their energy and to express the spirit of *ichigo ichie,* that is, wanting to fight perfectly each time for fear they will never have a second chance.

But no matter how important it is to win a bout, a judoist must realize that he is a member of society. His period of competition is short compared to the time that remains after his retirement. If he learns the habit of making diligent efforts, develops a never-say-die spirit, and adopts the attitude of *ichigo ichie* during his days as an active judoist, he will be able to put them to use when he becomes a full member of society. He must never end up merely as some "winning machine."

I have made many friends through judo, and my colleagues will remain like brothers to me no matter how many years elapse. The bond of our friendship has grown strong because we have concentrated all our energy on everything we have undertaken. As for my rivals in judo, because we gave our all in our bouts, I feel a certain type of friendship with them even today. I am no longer engaged in competitive judo, but my colleagues as well as my past rivals and I are cooperating with each other in various ways. I am confident that our friendships which were born from judo will become stronger and stronger as the days pass.

Judo, which has been my way of life, is, among all the Olympic events, the only sport to have developed in Japan. Judo bears the mark of Japanese culture, and is in fact a "sports culture" that Japan can take pride in. But there are numerous problems, both in Japan and abroad, which must be solved in order to further spread judo throughout the world. As a teacher of judo, it is my intention to develop promising judoists. At the same time, I intend to work on the various issues that confront judo with a never-say-die spirit.

Appendix: Judo Records

■ *World Judo Championships Records*

WEIGHT	1ST PLACE	2ND PLACE	3RD PLACE	
FIRST (Tokyo, 1956)				
Unclassified	Natsui (J)	Yoshimatsu (J)	Geesink (Neth.)	Courtine (France)
SECOND (Tokyo, 1958)				
Unclassified	Sone (J)	Kaminaga (J)	Yamashiki (J)	Pariset (France)
THIRD (Paris, 1961)				
Unclassified	Geesink (Neth.)	Sone (J)	Koga (J)	Kim (S. Korea)
FOURTH (Rio de Janeiro, 1965)				
68 kg. and under	Matsuda (J)	Minatoya (J)	Stepanov (USSR)	Park (S. Korea)
80 kg. and under	Okano (J)	Yamanaka (J)	Kim (S. Korea)	Bregman (USA)
Over 80 kg.	Geesink (Neth.)	Matsunaga (J)	Sakaguchi (J)	Rogers (Canada)
Unclassified	Inokuma (J)	Kibrosachwili (USSR)	Snijders (Neth.)	Kiknadze (USSR)
FIFTH (Salt Lake City, 1967)				
63 kg. and under	Shigeoka (J)	Matsuda (J)	Suslin (USSR)	Kim (S. Korea)
70 kg. and under	Minatoya (J)	Park, S. (S. Korea)	Nakatani (J)	Park, C. (S. Korea)
80 kg. and under	Maruki (J)	Poglajen (Neth.)	Enju (J)	Jacks (Brit.)
93 kg. and under	Sato, N. (J)	Sato, O. (J)	Eugster (Neth.)	Herrmann (W. Ger.)
Over 93 kg.	Ruska (Neth.)	Maejima (J)	Matsuzaka (J)	Kiknadze (USSR)
Unclassified	Matsunaga (J)	Glahn (W. Ger.)	Shinomaki (J)	Herrmann (W. Ger.)
SIXTH (Mexico City, 1969)				
63 kg. and under	Sonoda, Y. (J)	Nomura (J)	Kim, C. (S. Korea)	Suslin (USSR)
70 kg. and under	Minatoya (J)	Kono (J)	Rudmann (USSR)	Kim, B. (S. Korea)
80 kg. and under	Sonoda, I. (J)	Hiro (J)	Poklajen (Neth.)	Ip (S. Korea)
93 kg. and under	Sasahara (J)	Herrmann (W. Ger.)	Kawabata (J)	Pokatajen (USSR)
Over 93 kg.	Suma (J)	Glahn (W. Ger.)	Matsunaga (J)	Onashwili (USSR)
Unclassified	Shinomaki (J)	Ruska (Neth.)	Sato (J)	Eugster (Neth.)

WEIGHT	1ST PLACE	2ND PLACE	3RD PLACE	
	SEVENTH (Ludwigshafen, 1971)			
63 kg. and under	Kawaguchi (J)	Nomura (J)	Susllin (USSR)	Sam (S. Korea)
70 kg. and under	Tsuzawa (J)	Minatoya (J)	Hoetger (E. Ger.)	Zajkowski (Poland)
80 kg. and under	Fujii (J)	Shigematsu (J)	Starbrook (Brit.)	Auffray (France)
93 kg. and under	Sasahara (J)	Sato (J)	Ishii (Brazil)	Howiller (E. Ger.)
Over 93 kg.	Ruska (Neth.)	Glahn (W. Ger.)	Iwata (J)	Remfry (Brit.)
Unclassified	Shinomaki (J)	Kusnezov (USSR)	Sekine (J)	Glahn (W. Ger.)
	EIGHTH (Lausanne, 1973)			
63 kg. and under	Minami (J)	Kawaguchi (J)	Rodriguez (Cuba)	Pitschelauri (USSR)
70 kg. and under	Nomura (J)	Hoetger (E. Ger.)	Yoshimura (J)	Novikov (USSR)
80 kg. and under	Fujii (J)	Sonoda (J)	Reiter (Poland)	Look (E. Ger)
93 kg. and under	Sato (J)	Ueguchi (J)	Starbrook (Brit.)	Lorentz (E. Ger.)
Over 93 kg.	Takaki (J)	Nizharadze (USSR)	Novikov (USSR)	Remfry (Brit.)
Unclassified	Ninomiya (J)	Uemura (J)	Glahn (W. Ger.)	Zuckschwerdt (E. Ger.)
	NINTH (Vienna, 1975)			
63 kg. and under	Minami (J)	Kashiwazaki (J)	Reissman (E. Ger.)	Mariani (Italy)
70 kg. and under	Nevzorov (USSR)	Dvoinikov (USSR)	Kuramoto (J)	Akimoto (J)
80 kg. and under	Fujii (J)	Hara (J)	Adamczyk (Poland)	Coche (France)
93 kg. and under	Rouge (France)	Ishibashi (J)	Harshiladze (USSR)	Betanov (USSR)
Over 93 kg.	Endo (J)	Novikov (USSR)	Takaki (J)	Pak (N. Korea)
Unclassified	Uemura (J)	Ninomiya (J)	Chochoshvili (USSR)	Lorentz (E. Ger.)

WEIGHT	1ST PLACE	2ND PLACE	3RD PLACE	
ELEVENTH (Paris, 1979)				
60 Kg. and under	Rey (France)	Jong (Korea)	Moriwaki (J)	Mariani (Italy)
65 Kg. and under	Solodukhin (USSR)	Delvingt (France)	Palowski (Poland)	Sahara (J)
71 Kg. and under	Katsuki (J)	Gamba (Italy)	Adams (U.K.)	Namchalauri (USSR)
78 Kg. and under	Fujii (J)	Tchoullouyan (France)	Heinke (E. Ger.)	Park (Korea)
86 Kg. and under	Ultsch (E. Ger.)	Sanchis (France)	Carmona (Brazil)	Takahashi (J)
95 Kg. and under	Tkhubuluri (USSR)	Walle (Belgium)	Numan (Neth.)	Neureuther (W. Ger.)
Over 95 Kg.	Yamashita (J)	Rouge (France)	Varga (Hungary)	Kim (Korea)
Unclassified	Endo (J)	Kuznetsov (USSR)	Rouge (France)	Kovacevic (Yugoslavia)
TWELFTH (Maastricht, 1981)				
60 Kg. and under	Moriwaki (J)	Petrikov (Czech.)	Mariani (Italy)	Takahashi (Canada)
65 Kg. and under	Kashiwazaki (J)	Niculae (Rumania)	Ponomarev (USSR)	Hwang (Korea)
71 Kg. and under	Park (Korea)	Dyot (France)	Vujevic (Yugoslavia)	Lehman (E. Ger.)
78 Kg. and under	Adams (U.K.)	Kase (J)	Petrov (Bulgaria)	Doherty (Canada)
86 Kg. and under	Tchoullouyan (France)	Nose (J)	Ultsch (E. Ger.)	Bodaveli (USSR)
95 Kg. and under	Khubuluri (USSR)	Walle (Belgium)	Ha (Korea)	Vachon (France)
Over 95 Kg.	Yamashita (J)	Veritchev (USSR)	Kocman (Czech.)	Salonen (Finland)
Unclassified	Yamashita (J)	Reszko (Poland)	Walle (Belgium)	Oszvar (Hungary)
THIRTEENTH (Moscow, 1983)				
60 Kg. and under	Tletseri (USSR)	Bujko (Hungary)	Haráguchi (J)	Stollberg (E. Ger.)
65 Kg. and under	Solodukhin (USSR)	Matsuoka (J)	Pavlovski (Poland)	Rozati (Italy)
71 Kg. and under	Nakanishi (J)	Gamba (Italy)	Namgalauri (USSR)	Strahz (W. Ger.)
78 Kg. and under	Hikage (J)	Adams (U.K.)	Khabareli (USSR)	Fratica (Rumania)
86 Kg. and under	Ultsch (E. Ger.)	Canu (France)	Berland (USA)	Nose (J)
95 Kg. and under	Preschel (E. Ger.)	Divisenko (USSR)	Neureuther (W. Ger.)	Walle (Belgium)
Over 95 Kg.	Yamashita (J)	Wilhelm (Neth.)	Stohr (E. Ger.)	Cioc (Rumania)
Unclassified	Saito (J)	Kocman (Czech.)	Ozsvar (Hungary)	Walle (Belgium)

WEIGHT	1ST PLACE	2ND PLACE	3RD PLACE	
FOURTEENTH (Seoul, 1985)				
60 Kg. and under	Hosokawa (J)	Jupke (W. Ger.)	Khazret (USSR)	Bujko (Hungary)
65 Kg. and under	Sokoloy (USSR)	Lee (Korea)	Gawthorpe (U.K.)	Matsuoka (J)
71 Kg. and under	Ahn (Korea)	Swain (USA)	Stranz (W. Ger.)	Blach (Poland)
78 Kg. and under	Hikage (J)	Denhmigen (E. Ger.)	Adams (U.K.)	Vladimir (USSR)
86 Kg. and under	Seisebacher (Austria)	Petrov (Bulgaria)	Pesniak (USSR)	Canu (France)
95 Kg. and under	Sugai (J)	Ha (Korea)	Walle (Belgium)	Neureuther (W. Ger.)
Over 95 Kg.	Cho (Korea)	Saito (J)	Grigory (USSR)	Zaprianov (Bulgaria)
Unclassified	Masaki (J)	Rashwan (Egypt)	Wilhelm (Neth.)	Biktashev (USSR)

■ Olympic Judo Records

WEIGHT	1ST PLACE	2ND PLACE	3RD PLACE	
TOKYO (1964)				
68 Kg. and under	Nakatani (J)	Haenni (Switz.)	Stepanov (USSR)	Bogolubov (USSR)
80 Kg. and under	Okano (J)	Hofmann (W. Ger.)	Kim (S. Korea)	Bregman (USA)
Over 80 Kg.	Inokuma (J)	Rogers (Canada)	Kiknadze (USSR)	Chikviladze (USSR)
Unclassified	Geesink (Neth.)	Kaminaga (J)	Glahn (W. Ger.)	Boronovskis (Australia)
MUNICH (1972)				
63 Kg. and under	Kawaguchi (J)	Buidaa (Mongolia)	Mounier (France)	Kim (Korea)
70 Kg. and under	Nomura (J)	Zajkowski (Poland)	Novikov (USSR)	Hoetger (E. Ger.)
80 Kg. and under	Sekine (J)	Oh (Korea)	Coche (France)	Jacks (U.K.)
93 Kg. and under	Chochoshvili (USSR)	Starbrook (U.K.)	Barth (W. Ger.)	Ishii (Brazil)
Over 93 Kg.	Ruska (Neth.)	Glahn (W. Ger.)	Nishimura (J)	Onachvili (USSR)
Unclassified	Ruska (Neth.)	Kusnezov (USSR)	Parisi (U.K.)	Brondani (France)
MONTREAL (1976)				
63 Kg. and under	Rodriguez (Cuba)	Chang (Korea)	Tunosik (Hungary)	Mariani (Italy)
70 Kg. and under	Nevzorov (USSR)	Kuramoto (J)	Vial (France)	Taraj (Poland)
80 Kg. and under	Sonoda (J)	Dvoinikov (USSR)	Obadov (Yugoslavia)	Park (Korea)
93 Kg. and under	Ninomiya (J)	Harshiladze (USSR)	Starbrook (U.K.)	Roethlisberger (Switz.)
Over 93 Kg.	Novikov (USSR)	Neureuther (W. Ger.)	Coage (USA)	Endo (J)
Unclassified	Uemura (J)	Remfry (U.K.)	Chochoshvili (USSR)	Cho (Korea)
MOSCOW (1980)				
60 Kg. and under	Rey (France)	Rodriguez (Cuba)	Yemish (USSR)	Kincses (Hungary)
65 Kg. and under	Solodukhin (USSR)	Damdin (Mongolia)	Nedkov (Bulgaria)	Pawlowski (Poland)
71 Kg. and under	Gamba (Italy)	Adams (U.K.)	Lehmann (E. Ger.)	Davaadalai (Mongolia)
78 Kg. and under	Khabareli (USSR)	Ferrer (Cuba)	Heinke (E. Ger.)	Tchoullouyan (France)
86 Kg. and under	Röethlisberger (Switz.)	Azcuy (Cuba)	Ultsch (E. Ger.)	Yatskevich (USSR)
95 Kg. and under	Walle (Belgium)	Khubuluri (USSR)	Lorenz (E. Ger.)	Numan (Neth.)
Over 95 Kg.	Parisi (France)	Tsaprianov (Bulgaria)	Kovacevic (Yugoslavia)	Kocman (Czech.)
Unclassified	Lorenz (E. Ger.)	Parisi (France)	Ozsvar (Hungary)	Mapp (U.K.)

WEIGHT	1ST PLACE	2ND PLACE	3RD PLACE	
	LOS ANGELES (1984)			
60 Kg. and under	Hosokawa (J)	Kim (Korea)	Liddie (USA)	Eckersley (U.K.)
65 Kg. and under	Matsuoka (J)	Hwang (Korea)	Reiter (Austria)	Alexandre (France)
71 Kg. and under	Ahn (Korea)	Gamba (Italy)	Onmura (Brazil)	Brown (U.K.)
78 Kg. and under	Wieneke (W. Ger.)	Adams (U.K.)	Nowak (France)	Fratica (Rumania)
86 Kg. and under	Seisenbacher (Austria)	Berland (USA)	Nose (J)	Carmona (Brazil)
95 Kg. and under	Ha (Korea)	Vieira (Brazil)	Fridriksson (Israel)	Neureuther (W. Ger.)
Over 95 Kg.	Saito (J)	Parisi (France)	Cho (Korea)	Berger (Canada)
Unclassified	Yamashita (J)	Rashwan (Egypt)	Cioc (Rumania)	Schnabel (W. Ger.)

■ Women's World Judo Championships Records

WEIGHT	1ST PLACE	2ND PLACE	3RD PLACE	
	NEW YORK (1980)			
48 Kg. and under	Bridge (U.K.)	Denovellis (Italy)	Colignon (France)	Lewis (USA)
52 Kg. and under	Hrovat (Austria)	Yamaguchi (J)	McCarthy (U.K.)	Doger (France)
56 Kg. and under	Winklbauer (Austria)	Panza (France)	Doyle (U.K.)	Meulemans (Belgium)
61 Kg. and under	Staps (Neth.)	Toma (Italy)	Rottier (France)	Berg (W. Ger.)
66 Kg. and under	Simon (Austria)	Netherwood (U.K.)	Penick (USA)	Pierre (France)
72 Kg. and under	Triadou (France)	Classen (W. Ger.)	Meggelen (Neth.)	Malley (U.K.)
Over 72 Kg	Cal (Italy)	Fouillet (France)	Kieburg (W. Ger.)	Berghmans (Belgium)
Unclassified	Berghmans (Belgium)	Fouillet (France)	Classen (W. Ger.)	Fest (USA)
	PARIS (1982)			
48 Kg. and under	Briggs (U.K.)	Colignon (France)	Bink (Neth.)	Nakahara (J)
52 Kg. and under	Doyle (U.K.)	Yamaguchi (J)	Boyd (Australia)	Doger (France)
56 Kg. and under	Rodriguez (France)	Williams (Austria)	Aronoff (USA)	Bell (U.K.)
61 Kg. and under	Rottier (France)	Solheim (Norway)	Peeters (Belgium)	Ritschel (W. Ger.)
66 Kg. and under	Deydier (France)	Kruger (W. Ger.)	Andersen (Norway)	Staps (Neth.)
72 Kg. and under	Classen (W. Ger.)	Berghmans (Belgium)	Triadou (France)	Posch (Australia)
Over 72 Kg.	Lupino (France)	Castro (USA)	Unen (Neth.)	Motta (Italy)
Unclassified	Berghmans (Belgium)	Tateishi (J)	Sigmund (W. Ger.)	Triadou (France)
	VIENNA (1984)			
48 Kg. and under	Briggs (U.K.)	Colignon (France)	Anaya (USA)	Reardon (Austria)
52 Kg. and under	Yamaguchi (J)	Hrovat (Austria)	Boyd (Australia)	Majdan (Poland)
56 Kg. and under	Burns (USA)	Williams (Australia)	Winklbauer (Austria)	Arnaud (France)
61 Kg. and under	Hernandez (Venezuela)	Han (Neth.)	Rottier (France)	Hachinohe (J)
66 Kg. and under	Deydier (France)	Kok (Neth.)	Kandori (J)	Netherwood (U.K.)
72 Kg. and under	Berghmans (Belgium)	Classen (W. Ger.)	Staps (Neth.)	Vigneron (France)
Over 72 Kg.	Motta (Italy)	Gao (China)	Unen (Neth.)	Castro (USA)
Unclassified	Berghmans (Belgium)	Unen (Neth.)	Gao (China)	Lupino (France)

Glossary of Common Judo Terms

Definitions and translations for techniques discussed in the text appear in the two indexes.

aite: partner, opponent
ashi: foot, leg
atama: head

dojo: training hall

eri: collar, lapel

hara: stomach
hidari: left
hiji: elbow
hikite: pulling hand
hiza: knee

ippon: one point (in competition)

judogi: judo practice suit
judoka: judoist

kansetsu: joint
kata: shoulder; model technique
koka: less than a *yuko* (in competition)
koshi: hip
kubi: neck
kumikata: holding method
kuzure: modified (hold)

mae: forward, front
migi: right

momo: thigh
mune: chest

obi: belt (of *judogi*)

sensei: teacher, instructor
shiai: contest
shisei: posture
sode: sleeve

tatami: mat
te: hand, arm
tekubi: wrist
tokuiwaza: one's favorite or best technique
tsurite: lifting hand

ude: arm
ushiro: backward, rear

waki: armpit
waza: technique
waza ari: half point (in competition)

yoko: side
yubi: finger
yuko: less than a *waza ari* (in competition)
yusei gachi: win by judge's decision

General Index

Index of Judo Techniques

Arrows for combination techniques (*renrakuwaza*) indicate whether the technique in the main entry is applied to (→) or from (←) the technique in the subentry.

Nagewaza

1. ASHIWAZA

ashi guruma (leg whirl), 94
deashi barai (forward foot sweep), 48–51
harai tsurikomi ashi (pulling-lift leg sweep), 94
hiza guruma (knee whirl), 94
ko-soto gake (small outside hook), 94
ko-soto gari (small outside clip), 64–65
ko-uchi gari (small inside clip), 56–59
  ← *ippon seoi nage*, 154–55
  → *morote seoi nage*, 156–57
  ← *o-uchi gari*, 159
ko-uchi makikomi (small inner winding throw), 58–59
o-guruma (big whirl), 94
okuri ashi barai (assisting foot sweep), 52–53
o-soto gari (big outside clip), 66–67
  → *harai goshi*, 164–65
  ← *o-uchi gari*, 162
  → *sasae tsurikomi ashi*, 166–67
  → *ura nage*, 173
o-soto guruma (big outside whirl), 94
o-uchi gaeshi (big inside clip reversal)
  ← *o-uchi gari*, 174
o-uchi gari (big inside clip), 60–63
  → *kesa gatame*, 180
  → *ko-uchi gari*, 159
  → *morote seoi nage*, 158, 176
  → *o-soto gari*, 162
  → *o-uchi gaeshi*, 174
  → *tai otoshi*, 160, 161, 168–69, 170–71
  ← *tai otoshi*, 168–69
  → *uchimata*, 163
sasae tsurikomi ashi (supporting foot lifting-pull throw), 54–55
  → *kuzure kami shiho gatame*, 181
  ← *o-soto gari*, 166–67
  ← *tai otoshi*, 170–71
uchimata (inner-thigh reaping throw), 68–71
  ← *o-uchi gari*, 163
  → *sukui nage*, 175
  → *tai otoshi*, 177
  → *tani otoshi*, 188–89·

2. KOSHIWAZA

hane goshi (hip spring), 46–47
harai goshi (hip sweep), 42–45
  ← *o-soto gari*, 164–65
ko-tsuri goshi (small lifting hip throw), 93
o-goshi (hip roll), 36–37
o-tsuri goshi (big lifting hip throw), 93
sode tsurikomi goshi (lifting-sleeve-pull hip throw), 40–41

tsurikomi goshi (lifting-pull hip throw), 38–39
uki goshi (rising hip throw), 93
ushiro goshi (rear hip throw), 93
utsuri goshi (hip shift), 93
  ← *koshiwaza*, 172

3. MA SUTEMIWAZA

obitori gaeshi (belt-grab reversal), 80–81
sumi gaeshi (corner reversal), 95
tawara gaeshi (rice-bag reversal), 76–79
tomoe nage (round throw), 72–75
  → *ude hishigi juji gatame*, 182, 183
ura nage (rear throw), 95
  ← *o-soto gari*, 173

4. TEWAZA

ippon seoi nage (one-arm shoulder throw), 26–29
  → *ko-uchi gari*, 154–55
  → *okuri eri jime*, 186, 187
  → *yoko shiho gatame*, 178–79
kata guruma (shoulder whirl), 32–33
koshi guruma (hip whirl), 92
morote gari (two-arm clip), 92
morote seoi nage (two-arm shoulder throw), 30–31
  ← *ko-uchi gari*, 156–57
  ← *o-uchi gari*, 158, 176
sukui nage (scoop throw), 92
  ← *uchimata*, 175
sumi otoshi (corner drop), 92
tai otoshi (body drop), 24–25
  → *o-uchi gari*, 168–69
  ← *o-uchi gari*, 160, 161, 168–69, 170–71
  → *sasae tsurikomi ashi*, 170–71
  ← *uchimata*, 177
  → *ude hishigi juji gatame*, 184–85
uki otoshi (floating drop), 34–35

5. YOKO SUTEMIWAZA

hane makikomi (springing wrap-around throw), 96
hikikomi gaeshi (back-fall reversal), 88–91
soto makikomi (outside wrap-around throw), 96
tani otoshi (valley drop), 84–87
  ← *uchimata*, 188–89
  → *yoko shiho gatame*, 188–89
ukiwaza (floating throw), 82–83
yoko gake (side hook), 95
yoko guruma (side whirl), 96
yoko otoshi (side drop), 95
yoko wakare (side split), 96

Katamewaza